A JOYFUL NOISE

Thomas A. Dorsey "Father of Gospel" at Mahalia Jackson's grave, New Orleans   1970(2)/12   1981

A Joyful Noise

A Celebration of New Orleans Music

by Michael P. Smith

Introduction and Interviews by Alan Govenar

Taylor Publishing Company
Dallas, Texas

Copyright © 1990 by Michael P. Smith
Introduction and interviews copyright © 1990 by Alan Govenar

All rights reserved.

No parts of this book may be reproduced in any form
without written permission from the publisher.

Published by Taylor Publishing Company
          1550 West Mockingbird Lane
          Dallas, Texas 75235

Designed by SMITHERMANS
Library of Congress Cataloging-in-Publication Data

Smith, Michael P. (Michael Proctor), 1937–
   A Joyful Noise : A celebration of New Orleans music/by Michael P. Smith; Introduction and interviews by Alan Govenar.
     p. cm.
     ISBN 0-87833-664-8 : $24.95.—ISBN 0-87833-704-0 (soft) : $15.95
     1. Jazz music—Louisiana—New Orleans—Pictorial works. 2. Jazz musicians—Louisiana—New Orleans—Interviews. I. Title.
ML3508.8.N48S6 1990
781.65'09763'35—dc20
                                                                                  89-20635
                                                                                      CIP
                                                                                      MN

Printed in the United States of America

10 9 8 7 6 5 4 3 2 1

To *the* New Orleans Second Line

Make a joyful noise unto the Lord...
Psalm 98

Contents

Acknowledgments	XI
Introduction	1
Harold Dejan *Leader, Olympia Brass Band*	27
Allison "Tootie" Montana *Big Chief, Yellow Pocahontas tribe*	57
Johnny "Kool" Stephenson *Member, Scene Boosters Marching Club, Money Wasters Marching Club, Wild Magnolias Indian Club*	77
Sylvester Francis *Member, Gentlemen of Leisure Social & Pleasure Club/ Community Documentarian*	109
Larry Bannock *Chief, Golden Star Hunters Mardi Gras Indian tribe*	137
Lydia Gilford *Archbishop, Infant Jesus of Prague Spiritual Church of Christ*	153
E.J. Johnson *Archbishop, Israel Universal Divine Spiritual Churches of Christ*	163
A Personal Statement from the Photographer	203
Selected Bibliography	204

Acknowledgments

I would like to acknowledge my great indebtedness to the William Ransom Hogan Jazz Archives at Tulane University, where I was first employed as a photographer documenting New Orleans street music, where I learned the great value of this heritage, and where I continuously return to refresh my knowledge and understanding of the history of New Orleans music.

I would also like to express my thanks to the people and organizations I personally encountered along the way (and have been influenced by) who are devoted to our music and who have committed their lives to document, preserve, encourage, promote, and present traditional music and culture in New Orleans: Dr. William B. Russell, Richard Allen, Curt Jerde, and Bruce Raeburn at the William Ransom Hogan Jazz Archives; Alan and Sandra Jaffe, and all the folks at Preservation Hall; Quint Davis, Allison Miner and all the folks who established and continue the New Orleans Jazz & Heritage Festival and Foundation; Jim Isenogle and all the folks who established and maintain the Jean Lafitte National Historical Park (our nation's first living cultural heritage park); Dr. Clifton Johnson, Florence Borders and all the folks at the Amistad Research Center; Dr. Michael Sartisky and all the

folks at the Louisiana Endowment for the Humanities; Don Perry and the folks at the New Orleans Jazz Club; Eddie Edwards and the folks at the Louis Armstrong Foundation; Nick Spitzer, Bob Gates, Maida Bergeron and all the folks with the Louisiana Folklife Program; the City and State music commissions; Archbishop B.S. Johnson, Archbishop E.J. Johnson, Bishop Thomas Benjamin Watson, Bishop Lydia Guilford and all the leaders and members of the Spiritual Churches of New Orleans; Harold Dejan and Milton Batiste, leaders of the Olympia Brass Band; Greg Stafford, leader of the Young Tuxedo Brass Band; Herbert McCarver, leader of the Pin Stripe Brass Band; Kermit Ruffins and Philip Frazer, leaders of the Rebirth Jazz Band; Anthony Lacen and Benny Jones, leaders of the Chosen Few Brass Band; all the traditional brass bands and musicians presently working the streets and clubs of the city: Big Chief, Wild Tchoupitoulas, George "Jolly" Landry; Big Chief, Black Eagles, Percy "Pete" Lewis; Big Chief, Golden Star Hunters, Larry E. Bannock; Big Chief, White Cloud Hunters, Charles Taylor; Big Chief, White Eagles, Gerald "Jake" Millon; Big Chief, Yellow Pocahontas, Tootie Montana; Big Chief, 9th Ward Hunters, Rudy Bougere; Big Chief, Wild Magnolias, Bo Dollis; Big Chief, Guardians of the Flame, Donald Harrison, Sr., and others; Lionel Oubichon, Darrell Johnson, "Flag," "Bubble," "House," "Bird," and others among the Mardi Gras Indian gangs who have opened their minds and hearts to me; Alan Lomax, John Broven, Sam Charters, Ben Sandmel, Al and Diana Rose, Andrew Kaslow, Claude Jacobs, Joe Logsdon, Joe Guillottee, Jeff Hannusch, Tad Jones, Jason Berry, Lynn Abbott, Don Marquis, Kalamu Ya Salaam, William J. Schafer, "Blue Lu," Danny Barker and others who have supported or written profoundly about our music and street culture; Cosimo Matassa, Mary Ledbetter and the folks with the New Orleans Music and Entertainment Association; Cyril Neville and the folks with New Orleans Music Organized; Rev. Simmie Harvie, Ron Chisom, Jim Hayes, Badi Murphy, Norman Smith and other activitists dedicated to community priorities and heritage; Jerome Smith and the Tamborine & Fan Club, Randy Mitchell and the Treme Birthright Society and Development Corporation, and other community activist associations; Thelma Jones, Herbert Gettridge, Frank Charles III, Ashton Ramsey, Lionel Batiste, Joe Bernard, Phillip Clay, Norman Dixon, Peter Goines, Jessie Hill, Shannon Powell, Morris Bachemin, Benny Jones, "Bubble," "Dut," "Hot,"

"Eyes," "Toe Toe," "Stinky," "Ratty," "Mr. Google-Eyes," "Spike," "Tuba," "Ice Cream," and other street friends: especially Johnny "Kool" Stephenson and Sylvester Francis, who document the culture from within; and last but not least among individuals who are a part of this second-line community, Mike Stark, Jules Cahn, Betty "Big Mama" Rankin, Mary Louise "Mike" Trammell, Karen Snyder, Nancy Ochsenschlager, Walter and Jerry Brock (cofounders of WWOZ 90.7FM radio, dedicated to New Orleans music). Steve Armbruster, Henry Drevich, Thorny Penfield, Gloria Powers, Joe Louis Caldwell, and the many other supporters and well-wishers in the passing parade too numerous to mention—all of whom contribute greatly to the continuation of our living cultural heritage.

It is important to acknowledge also the contributions of the neighborhood music clubs: Darrell's Bar & Lounge, the Patio Lounge, the Glass House, Dorothy's Medallion, Winnie's, Jerry's, Lu & Charlie's, the Dew Drop, the H&R Bar, the Caldonia, Greasy's, the Hollow Point, Tee Bert's Lounge, Two Jacks, Benny's, Tyler's, Tipitina's, Snug Harbor, and the many other clubs and bars presenting and supporting the real music of New Orleans, usually at great expense. These small clubs are "nesting" places for our musicians, where they jam for local audiences and search for new sounds and musical ideas to take out into the larger world.

The street parades, sponsored by the traditional social and benevolent organizations of New Orleans, the Mardi Gras Indian gangs, the neighborhood bars and music clubs, and the vernacular churches constitute the "wetlands" for New Orleans jazz—the authentic cultural environment from which almost all of the traditional New Orleans music grows.

George Lewis funeral   171/24   1969

Introduction

by Alan Govenar

In New Orleans when a member of a traditional African-American or Creole community dies, friends, family, and even strangers participate in a unique cultural celebration which lasts for days. Musicians and friends join the family at home to mourn and to offer help during this difficult time. At the wake the night before the funeral, they gather in large numbers to play music while friends and family testify about their faith and share their memories of the deceased. Relatives and friends stay with the bereaved family all night. In the morning, after a short dismissal service at the funeral home, the body is transferred to the church in a solemn walking procession. On this march the brass bands play a number of gospel dirges and favorite hymns, such as "Just A Closer Walk With Thee" or "Bye and Bye." A brass band or large group of musicians leads the procession, and the dirge continues with a sad, almost moaning tone, the drums setting the cadence until the grand marshall or bandleader signals for them to prepare for entry into the church. At the church the band, along with an honor guard, lines up on each side of the steps. Pallbearers carry the casket past the brass band and the honor guard into the church, where friends of the deceased, members of the various

A Joyful Noise

fraternal, social, and business organizations, and people from the community have congregated. The casket is opened at the front of the church for final viewing and the service proceeds for an hour or more with eulogies, hymns, testimonies, and prayers. Toward the end of the service the musicians may also come in and play their eulogy as they pass slowly by the coffin.

By the time the church service ends, several hundred more people have gathered in the street. Musicians lead the procession out of the church and the pallbearers follow behind carrying the casket. While they lift the casket into the hearse, a brass band may play an old hymn like "Take Your Burden to the Lord." As the band leaves, the cadence is slow and mournful. Sometimes, nowadays, the procession continues for only a few blocks before the funeral director signals for the body to be "cut away" or "turned loose." The musicians and the crowd part and the funeral procession passes in between. Well-wishers "touch the hearse good-bye." Then the hearse and all the cars behind it accelerate and head toward the cemetery. Today, the old cemeteries in the central part of New Orleans are expensive, and families more often use those on the outskirts. Sometimes the brass bands will follow the hearse in a bus and play at the gravesite, then return to the community and resume the parade, which might go on for hours, visiting the favorite bars of the deceased and stopping at the family home. However, some of the older fraternal organizations have large crypts or family tombs in the inner city cemeteries, and the funeral proceeds directly from the church to the burial ground, where the body is laid to rest.

After the body is "cut away" or placed in the crypt, the mood of the parade changes from sadness to celebration. The brass bands break into jazz and usually play the favorite tunes of the deceased. They may also play the deceased's own compositions. Attending dignitaries from the Second Line clubs, black Indian gangs, and other traditional groups following the bands pick up the tempo and move to the syncopations of the music in a style unique to New Orleans. In his memoirs, Baby Dodds, a well-known New Orleans drummer, wrote, "We'd play the same popular numbers that we used to play with dance bands.... It became a tradition to play jazzy numbers going back to make the relatives and friends cast off their sadness. And the people along the streets used to dance to the

A Celebration of New Orleans Music

George Lewis funeral   174/22   1969

Roosevelt Sykes at the New Orleans Jazz & Heritage Festival   838/7   1973

music.... The jazz played after New Orleans funerals didn't show any lack of respect for the person being buried. It rather showed their people that we wanted them to be happy." In these funeral processions are the roots of jazz and the continuation of a tradition in which life is affirmed after death is honored.

New Orleans brass bands have been an important influence in the development of jazz since its beginnings, and have provided instrumentation, instrumental techniques, and repertoire. In the nineteenth century, brass bands played for the military, circuses, carnivals, minstrel and medicine shows, political rallies, churches, picnics, dances, athletic contests, and holiday gatherings. Numerous African-American brass bands were formed in New Orleans after the Civil War and during Reconstruction. Many of these bands were self-schooled and performed in the streets. "Habits and attitudes of brass bandsmen carried into jazz," historian William Schafer observed, "shaping its music for decades after it was apparently dissociated from the military tradition." African-American brass bands in New Orleans, however, developed their own distinctive performance styles.

Among African-Americans in New Orleans, brass bands have retained a multifunctional significance and are an important component of community-based events and traditional celebrations. Harold Dejan, leader of the Olympia Brass Band, one of the oldest active brass bands in New Orleans, estimates that fifteen marching brass bands still actively perform at funerals, picnics, and at the annual parades hosted by traditional social organizations in the African-American communities. Usually there are eight to ten formal members in each of the marching bands, including two trumpets, two trombones, a sousaphone or tuba, snare drum, bass drum, cymbal, and sometimes clarinet, and alto and tenor saxophones. Many others bring their own percussion instruments to accompany the bands in the street. Over the last two decades a resurgence of interest in New Orleans brass bands has helped to spawn a new generation of jazz musicians who are committed to carrying into new dimensions the traditional musical styles. The music continues to evolve in response to changes in popular music and community and audience context. The best known of the younger bands, the Dirty Dozen Brass Band, the Rebirth Brass Band, and the Chosen Few, combine traditional brass repertory with Afro-Caribbean percussion and other musical styles of the day—jazz, rhythm and

A JOYFUL NOISE

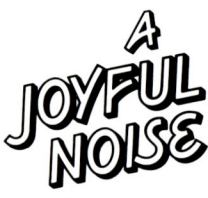

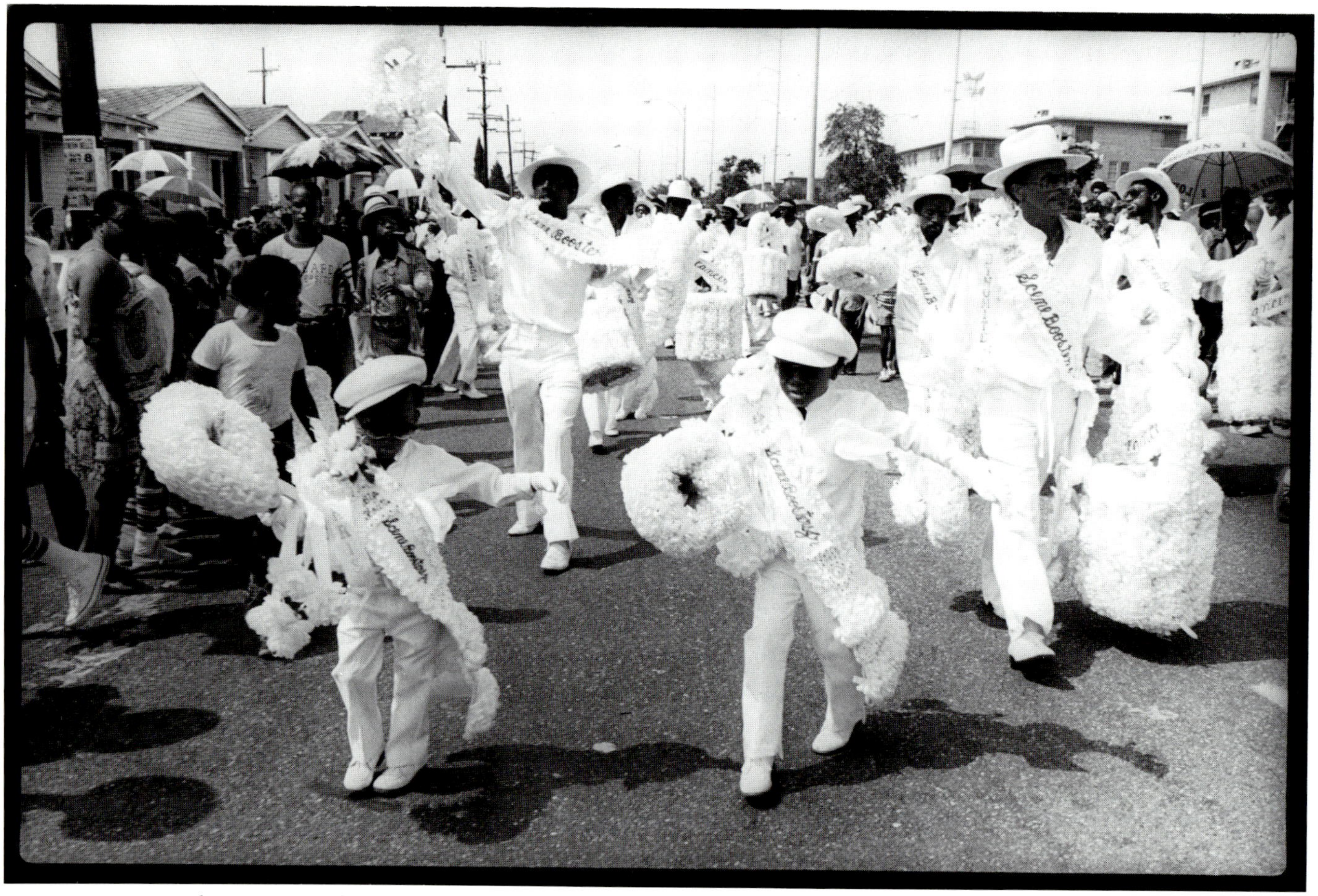

Scene Boosters Social & Pleasure Club annual parade 1660/28A 1978

blues, bebop, gospel, and pop. The arrangements are free-form and improvised to suit the occasion.

On almost every Sunday from late August to mid-May—all but the hottest days of summer—marching brass bands lead parades of all kinds and represent an enormous underdeveloped cultural and economic resource for the city. Parades are planned by churches, social aid and pleasure clubs, marching clubs, Indian gangs, and other traditional organizations. The parades honor a variety of occasions including Martin Luther King Day, Black History Month, Mardi Gras, St. Joseph's Night, and Mother's Day, to name but a few. Today, New Orleans parades are limited to four hours by city ordinance, but they are nonetheless traditional and are similar to the parades described by Louis Armstrong in his autobiography.

"All the members wore full dress uniforms and with those beautiful silk ribbons streaming from their shoulders they were a magnificent sight. At the head of the parade rode the aides in full dress suits and mounted on fine horses with ribbons around their heads. The brass band followed, shouting a hot swing march as everyone jumped for joy. The members of the club marched behind wearing white felt hats, white silk shirts (the very best silk), and mohair trousers. When all the clubs paraded it took nearly all day to see them pass, but one never got tired watching."

Social and fraternal organizations proliferated after Emancipation. They were formally incorporated in the 1880s as mutual aid and benevolent societies in an effort to legally protect rights to property gained during Reconstruction, to ensure the well-being of their members, and to provide proper burial. At the turn of the century, historian Claude Jacobs estimates that "four-fifths of the local (black) population belonged to benevolent societies... more than any other types of voluntary associations except churches." In the records of the Girod Street Cemetery and Saint Louis Cemetery Number Two alone, Jacobs found references to the tombs built by approximately two hundred benevolent societies. The benevolent societies provided the "major form of social security against sickness, death, and poverty. They aided orphan asylums, Negro veterans, and the indigent, gave religious education to children, and fought against segregation and for racial uplift."

Since their beginnings, these social and benevolent organizations have

been broadly involved in the traditional life of the African-American communities, but they are visible to outsiders only during the annual parades. On the day of an annual parade or "banner blessing," the club members gather in the early morning for breakfast ceremonies and then move to the community church. The march starts by midday and, over the course of four hours, covers a route of ten to twelve miles through the African-American neighborhoods. The celebration usually ends with a club-sponsored dinner and ball. The number of bands in the parade varies with the size of the club and the funds available. Preparations for a parade and the various celebrations and services of a club are a year-round activity that begins in family tradition but extends far into the community.

The end of August in New Orleans may be hot and humid, but the parades usually overcome the severity of the weather and the restrictions imposed by a worsening economy. A tropical thunderstorm may interrupt the marching, but the parade continues as soon as the rain lets up. The leaders occupy the positions of honor at the front of the first division. Officers of the clubs wear elaborate, individually-made ribbons or sashes that bear their titles. One member carries a banner that identifies the club, with the dates of its founding and incorporation. Within each division is a marching band followed by the members with color-coordinated suits, shirts, ties, baskets, fans, and shoes (outfits costing from $500 to $2,500 each). The members are flanked and followed by younger men, women, and children. With a signal and a shrill whistle from the Grand Marshall, a marching brass band starts up and the "Second Liners" jump in. The Second Liners come mostly from the black neighborhoods around the city and have their own individualistic dress that includes everything from fancy costumes to T-shirts and tank tops, jeans and shorts, high top sneakers and walking shoes.

African-American parades in New Orleans are distinctly different from parades held anywhere else in North America. Most of the viewers become participants, moving through the streets, dancing from one division to another, comparing the bands or the "dress" of the club members. The strutting, dancing, and intricate body movements of these Second Liners are an expressive language with African roots that are only beginning to be analyzed by scholars.

A typical large parade has five or six bands and divisions, each with two

A Celebration of New Orleans Music

Duke Ellington & Mahalia Jackson at the New Orleans Jazz & Heritage Festival   359/31A   1970

Reborn in the name of Jesus, Beauty of Holiness Spiritual Church   1176/34A   1974

or three hundred people intimate with the marching organization, and a second line contingent of five hundred to a thousand from the surrounding communities who support the traditional culture. In sum, the parade may involve four or five thousand people, with many more coming out of their houses and local businesses along the parade route to watch. Over the course of the afternoon the parade stops at special neighborhood bars and watering holes, where the marchers and principal second liners are treated to drinks, sandwiches, and snacks.

At the very front of today's parades is a City of New Orleans police vehicle. Scattered alongside are mounted police. The relations between the paraders and the police are obviously strained, as evidenced by a mix of emotions—disdain, amusement, concern, and anger. Unfortunately, the parades are often considered a nuisance by the police and by some city officials.

The cost of organizing social aid and pleasure club parades continues to escalate. Johnny "Kool" Stephenson, a longstanding member of the Scene Boosters and Money Wasters marching clubs, says that the cost of the mandatory police security has risen from two hundred and sixty dollars in the 1970s to more than sixteen hundred dollars in the 1980s. These increased costs, combined with rising unemployment, have caused some of the marching clubs to cut back—buying less expensive suits and curtailing their annual parades. At present there are approximately fifty marching, social, and fraternal organizations in the city, and about fifteen have parades. Each year the leaders of the clubs meet to decide on the parade schedule, and begin planning to acquire permits and book the bands.

The roots of these community parades and celebrations of music and dance date back to the earliest years of the city of New Orleans and have African antecedents. People of African descent have been in New Orleans, like the French, from the early eighteenth century. The city's relative social and geographic isolation during its early history as a French colony and international port contributed to the unique black culture. Blacks were brought to the city as slaves from Senegal, Senegambia, and the Windward Coast of West Africa, as well as from the French Caribbean islands, especially Haiti, after the French Revolution. Some were trained as skilled laborers and craftsmen and were able to buy freedom for themselves

A Joyful Noise

and their families upon enactment of the so-called Code Noire, which made this possible for the first time. This gave rise to a community known as the "Freemen of Color." The intermarriage of Freemen of Color with native Indians and French settlers resulted in the growth of Creoles—blacks of mixed ancestry. The cultural composition of New Orleans was complicated further by an eighteenth-century Spanish era and an influx of Anglo-Americans following the Louisiana Purchase.

From the earliest days of the city, New Orleans slaves were allowed to gather on Sundays on the "Congo Plains," an area outside the city ramparts. In 1817, the New Orleans City Council moved to "corral" the "practices" of the slaves, so that they could be better controlled by the police. City authorities feared the influx of voodoo that stemmed, in part, from the migration of Africans fleeing the Caribbean and the Haitian Revolution. The city forbade the gathering of slaves for any reason except on Sunday in the Congo Plains, which was later more narrowly defined as Congo Square. The last remnant of that square is now the area between Municipal Auditorium and North Rampart Street, adjacent to Louis Armstrong Park. Ironically, the ordinance designed to contain the practices of the slaves placed these cultural celebrations at the center of attention. Congo Square became one of the most popular spots in the city, and descriptions of music and dance written by "outsiders" abound, although they constitute only a limited and shallow look at what was going on.

African cultural celebrations and gatherings in the Congo Plains continued until the enactment of the infamous Jim Crow laws in 1875, which severely limited the rights of blacks and banished them from public parks in New Orleans. This discrimination forced many of the political and cultural activities of blacks underground, into the ghettos and outlying sections of the city.

Jim Crow laws began an era marked by the breakdown of African tribal identities and the loss of African language and culture. The cultures of Africa cross-fertilized with the European, Latin, and native cultures in all parts of the New World. Soon after the passing of Jim Crow laws the "gangs," which had been banished from Congo Square, re-formed with the names of Indian tribes in the black neighborhoods. There blacks gathered to continue the dances, songs, drumming, and celebration which had been made illegal in public. The gangs took the

A Celebration of New Orleans Music

Ellyna Tatum's funeral   2477/5   1986

A JOYFUL NOISE

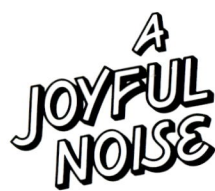

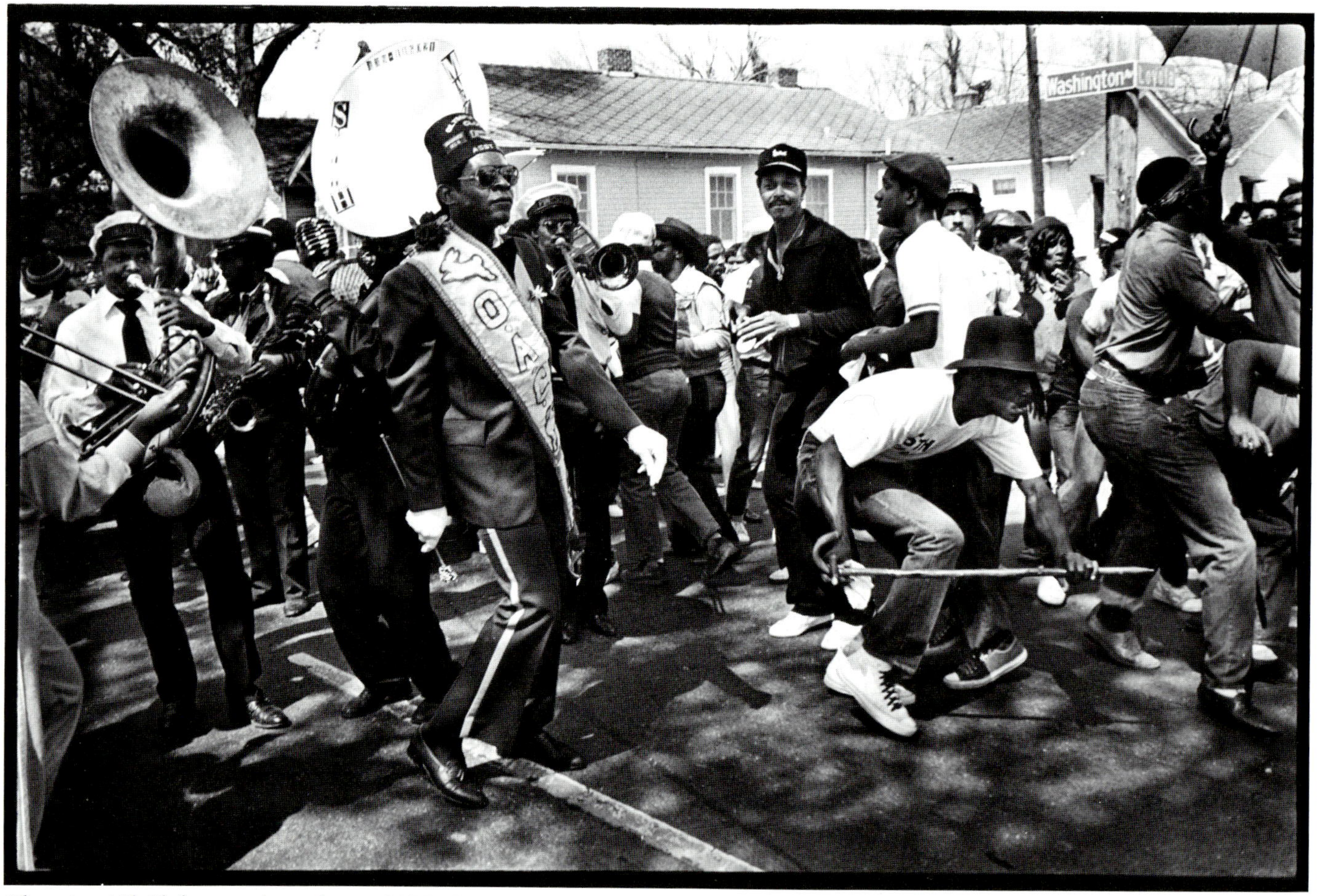

Olympian Aid Club, annual parade 2185/13 1983

names and costumes of Indian tribes because the Indians had helped the slaves as well as the Reconstruction-era blacks. There are different theories about the origins of the black Indian gangs. One of the first tribes, the Creole Wild West, appears to have been influenced by Plains Indians who performed in Buffalo Bill's Wild West Show, in 1884 and 1885.

Allison "Tootie" Montana, Big Chief of the Yellow Pocahontas tribe since 1949, recalls hearing about the Creole Wild West from his grandmother, Jeanne Durrell, who was the sister of Becate Batiste, the Chief of the Creole Wild West tribe in the 1880s. Tootie's father, Alfred Montana, was Chief of the Yellow Pocahontas tribe in the 1930s and 1940s. Tootie says he is a "Creole with mixed ancestry and part Indian. My grandmother said that we had Indian blood. If you'd seen her, you could tell. She lived to be ninety-eight and she told me about the Indians and my granduncle Batiste and how the other Indian tribes were formed after him."

Today there are an estimated thirty black Indian tribes in the city of New Orleans, although the exact number varies from year to year. They march and parade on different days around Mardi Gras and spend thousands to remake their costumes every year using different color feathers, plumes, and hand-sewn patches. Mardi Gras and St. Joseph's Night are considered marches because they involve spontaneous and unpermitted processions through the streets. Super Sunday, when all the Indian tribes assemble together, is called a parade because it is formally permitted and has police security.

In 1987 Tootie Montana became the first Mardi Gras Indian to receive a National Heritage Fellowship from the National Endowment for the Arts. Montana's hard-won success exemplifies the aspirations and struggles of his generation. In a letter of support for Montana's nomination, photographer Michael P. Smith wrote, "Chief Allison Montana is seen as the greatest living spirit carrying these valuable traditions into the future. The Mardi Gras Indians are certainly the most significant traditional culture in New Orleans. They are at the base of the largest ethnic population in the area. They have made seminal contributions to traditional jazz, brass marching bands, rhythm and blues, and cultural celebration in the city, although they have remained isolated and unrecognized to the present."

Segregation and discrimination in New Orleans has led to a matrix of social,

Blackhawk Service at Infant Jesus of Prague Spiritual Church   1358/8A   1975

political, and economic problems. But they have also spawned a cultural autonomy in the black communities which is manifest in the Indian gangs as well as in the various social and fraternal organizations, marching jazz bands, neighborhood parades, and church ceremonies. Within the city, however, there is a history of competition and rivalries among Creole and American blacks in the different neighborhoods. Moreover, as poet and critic Kalamu Ya Salaam asserts, people of African descent were forced to accept Americanization and to hide their culture from public view. This contributed to the misinterpretation of African-American culture by observers and suppressed the transmission of this culture among African-Americans themselves.

In fact, each of the black neighborhoods of New Orleans has distinctive social and fraternal organizations, and bands, as well as Indian tribes. The styles of costume, music, and dance progress creatively from year to year, but are rooted in traditions—traditions practiced largely in community celebrations. The black Indian tribes, for example, did not begin to gain broad public recognition until the first annual New Orleans Jazz and Heritage Festival in 1970, when the Golden Eagles, the Wild Magnolias, and other groups along with marching jazz bands were presented.

Since 1970 the black Indian tribes, as well as the brass bands and second liners, have been acclaimed at festivals throughout the United States and abroad. In Ascona, Switzerland, there is even a fifteen-year-old festival devoted entirely to New Orleans music. In recent years the documentation of African-American culture in New Orleans has increased significantly.

One of the most respected documenters is photographer Michael P. Smith. Since 1968, Smith has captured many facets of this urban cultural life, including social, fraternal, and marching club parades of a number of ethnic communities, jazz funerals, ceremonies in Spiritualist churches, Indian gangs and practices, and featured performers at every New Orleans Jazz and Heritage Festival.

Smith says, "What motivated me to document and preserve images and information about the traditional music communities of New Orleans were the historical circumstances and my fundamental interest in music.

"When I first discovered the camera in the mid-1960s, I photographed

Chief "Pete" Percy Lewis (Black Eagles Mardi Gras Indian Tribe) New Orleans Jazz & Heritage Festival   1447/15   1977

indiscriminantly. I photographed anything—houses, people, landscapes, objects—things as themselves. Then in the late '60s I photographed events—jazz funerals, love-ins, demonstrations, people relating to each other and to their cultural environment. But these pictures, while some contained energy, held little magic. They did not interact with the imagination.

"Then I began to understand the power of photography to reach beyond naturalistic meaning into the realm of the spirit, to lift something out of its natural surroundings and strip it of its camouflage. I started to observe the little ways in which things are inadvertently revealed. I became intrigued by façades, masking, cultural celebration, and the various ways things and people present themselves to the world, sometimes diabolical little things which might go unnoticed but for the magic of the camera."

What unifies the photography of Michael P. Smith is its emphasis upon the quality of life and the power of perception. Smith mediates his position as an outsider through his commitment. He is at once documentarian of and advocate for his subjects. In so doing he focuses attention on the importance of cultural preservation, and demonstrates his ability to gain and maintain access to his subjects, to develop an understanding of their world view, and to translate that understanding into visual imagery.

Since the 1960s, Smith has worked with community leaders and made copies of his photos available to his subjects. Larry Bannock, Chief of the Golden Star Hunters Indian tribe, says, "Mike Smith was the first white photographer to come back, to bring us copies, to talk to us and try to help us with our problems with the city."

Smith is ethnographic in his approach to photography and emphasizes the structure and organization of what he is seeing. "I hear about an event and I go there. I photograph compulsively as a documenter/collector of visual information. I may go a year or more without printing or analyzing certain areas of my work, but I do make contact sheets and review everything. I make notations to identify the event and I always print a few of my best images to give to the people in them. I realize the importance of feedback in the community and of keeping a good visual record of these things to aid in bringing about their recognition and development."

While he is working, Smith says, "I want to be as invisible with my camera as I can, to eliminate everything that's not essential in transmitting the essence of the moment. I'm always hoping for a very precise composition, balancing maximum information with artistic composition to achieve maximum impact. I'm very much watching everything."

The compositions of Smith's photographs are instantaneous and often unpredictable. "Everything in the picture should contribute to it in terms of composition, balance, texture, and meaning," he says. "I don't think of technical things that much. It's the image and the essence of what I'm looking at that's primary. I'm fully aware of not just what I'm seeing, but what I'm hearing, the way people are responding to the music or the moment and relating to the event."

Smith has gradually become more discerning in his choice of subjects. He tends to feature individuals and groups who have had significant impact on their communities. In covering an event Smith begins to "close in and circle" to tighten his composition. He never knows which image in the various series he shoots at any event will be the best. Over the course of a four-hour parade, for example, Smith usually shoots eight to ten, thirty-six-exposure rolls of film.

In printing, Smith never crops the image. He prints the picture full-frame with a heavy black border that results from the bleed through of light around the filed edges of the negative carrier. In this way the print reflects the maximum information on the negative. He intensifies the photographic quality of the image through selenium toning, which changes the feeling of the black tones.

The heavy black borders in Smith's printing accentuate the limits of possibility in photography and in social change. Throughout his career Smith has been committed to the preservation of what he calls "the cultural wetlands," the breeding ground of New Orleans music. "I realized very quickly," Smith says of his work in the black community, "I was photographing not only a phenomenal culture, but a severely repressed culture. When I would talk to people outside the culture about it they didn't understand what I was talking about. They couldn't really picture the grandeur and importance of these parades. They'd heard of jazz funerals, for example, but couldn't conceive of the magnitude of the annual social

A Celebration of New Orleans Music

Dancing in the Rain, Young Men's Olympian annual parade, Mellow Fellows division
2410/37   1985

A JOYFUL NOISE

Spencer Coudray funeral   2265/24A   1983

Interior analogies   640/2   1972

A Celebration of New Orleans Music

"Give the people what they want"   1976

Rebirth Jazz Band at the New Orleans Jazz & Heritage Festival   2697/9   1988

A Celebration of New Orleans Music

and pleasure club parades. Nearly all of New Orleans music and folklife are connected and nourished by these unique religious traditions and public celebrations. But great changes are taking place. Without help these traditions will die out."

Smith began making color slides in the mid-1970s, to show at City Hall and to illustrate to large audiences how the parades have changed over the years and how they are threatened by ignorance and racial discrimination. "It was my appreciation of the music and the culture that produced my documentation," he explains, "but it was my awareness of the repression of that culture that made me want to do something about it. I witnessed the problems when I first began, but it has taken years to have any impact on the situation. There is just beginning to be an interest and appreciation of the black cultural celebrations outside the black communities. But even within the black communities there are problems understanding the larger value of the parades to the history of New Orleans music and the future economic development of the city."

The photography of Michael Smith is direct, vital, and personal, charged with respect and the ecstatic energy of experience. His photographs are arranged in chronological order (for the most part) and were selected on the basis of the content, context, and integrity of the images, people, and celebrations represented. Also included are interviews with some of the people in the photographs. Together, the photographs and interviews underscore the diversity of the African-American communities in the city and are a tribute to a generation of New Orleans music.

A JOYFUL NOISE

Percy Lewis, "Big Chief Pete," Mardi Gras Indian Gang, at home   1725/10   1979

Harold Dejan

(*Leader, Olympia Brass Band*)

My earliest memories of brass bands in New Orleans are that they used to play everywhere—picnics, parties, dances—and they always had their uniforms on. They marched in parades and funerals and they wore the same outfits when they played a dance.

    I grew up in New Orleans between the Treme and the Seventh Ward, on Roman between St. Anne and Dumaine, born February 4, 1909. My brother studied violin with Professor Nickelson and later took up trumpet. My little sister played piano, but she stopped. We used to take lessons from Professor Nickelson, who was living on Galvez between Iberville and Canal. We were paying a dollar a lesson back then. Professor Nickelson was a concert violinist and he had a daughter who was a concert pianist. He didn't like jazz and we had to stick to that concert music. I was waiting for Lorenzo Tio to come back from Chicago. So, I asked my daddy if I could take lessons with somebody else until Lorenzo Tio came back. I wanted to play jazz. I was about nine or ten years old at that time. And while Lorenzo Tio was gone, Frank Crump helped me. He was a clarinetist and saxophonist. Then my brother wanted to play trumpet and daddy bought him a

Paul Barbarin funeral, St. Louis Cemetery #2   194/23   1969

trumpet and we went to Professor Chilgnee. He charged twenty-five cents a lesson. He'd write you a theory book for twenty-five cents, write his own method in a music book, write the scales and everything out. He didn't go to the music store. He did it all himself, in beautiful handwriting. You couldn't miss him. He was a postman. He used to carry mail in the day, and in the evening we'd go to his house and take our lesson.

There used to be gangs on the streets and the fellows would stop us and say, "Play me something." And I'd say, "Oh, I can't play nothing. I just learned to play the scale today." And they'd say, "Well, play the scale," and we had to take our horns out and play the scale and they'd let us go.

I started first with the Holy Ghost Brass Band. We used to make trips to Opelousas and places like that. That's when I was playing E-flat clarinet. Lorenzo Tio had told my dad, "If you get him an E-flat clarinet, I'll put him with the Holy Ghost Brass Band." So my daddy bought me that clarinet and I played funerals and parades.

I played with several brass bands. I had many opportunities to play with the Imperial Brass Band, one of the best. I asked them why they carried two saxophones instead of a clarinet. I wanted to know because every brass band had clarinets. They said, "You look up the history of music. Saxophone is a brass instrument and this is a brass band." There are ten pieces in a brass band.

I started with clarinet. I used to go to hear Sam Morgan play, and I liked to hear Earl Forchette on saxophone. He was one of the best soprano and alto players I ever heard. He and Albert Nicholas inspired me to take up saxophone. The first clarinets I heard in the brass band were Willie Humphrey and Lorenzo Tio.

Barry Martin came here one time and I was playing with Miner's Brass Band. He said, "I've been listening to a lot of the brass bands and I'd like to record you. Do you have your own brass band?"

I said, "Yeah, I carry the No. 2 Eureka."

He said, "I'll record you if you change the name of the band. I don't like the No. 2."

I said, "I played with the Olympia when I was a teenager. And the Olympia Brass goes back to 1883, and I think that the oldest name is the best because I

Paul Barbarin funeral, Albert Walters, Jack Willis, Ernie Cagnolatti   190/22A   1969

intend to keep the tradition going." So he recorded me. Louis Keppard was on sousaphone, Freddie Keppard on first trumpet, Buddy Petit on second trumpet.

The Olympia Brass Band was one of the first that was organized. I understand that there was, however, a tradition of brass bands before that, but they were not as organized. I try to keep my brass band as close to tradition as possible. Sometimes we'll be out on the street, playing for one of the Social and Pleasure Clubs, and they'll ask for a number. If we know it, we're going to play it for them, but we keep close to the tradition, "Panama Rag," "Olympia on Parade," "Olympia Special," "Bugle Call Rag," "Bugle Boy." I made the record "Lord, Lord" with a number of my oldest friends back in 1956, and I've always used that number as my theme song because the Lord has always been good to me.

That New Orleans beat came from those freed slaves that went to Congo Square on Sunday evenings. They used to play that good rhythm and drums. People like Buddy Bolden, old man Humphrey, and Paul Barbarin, Louis Cottrell—they picked up on that.

When I was growing up I remember the Mardi Gras Indians, the Yellow Pocahontas tribe, the Red, White, and Blues. I'd follow them for about a block or something, but they used to do a lot of fighting, one tribe against another.

There's still a drumming tradition that's maintained by the Indian tribes. Whenever you have a brass band playing in the street in New Orleans, the folks that are behind the drum section with the cowbells and the tambourines and the sticks are from the tribes.

All during the year, a lot of the Indians follow the brass bands in the streets. I guess they get the exercise for Carnival or something like that. That's the way I figure it. Tootie Montana, the Chief of the Yellow Pocahontas—most everywhere we play, a funeral or parade, he's right there.

A lot of people don't recognize it's the Indians that the back beat comes from. Without that bass drum it's sad. Henry Booker T. Glass, who was the bass drummer for the Olympia Brass Band, was extremely good. He also masked with the Yellow Pocahontas for a long time. He was kind of rough himself. He carried a .45 in his bosom. He was scared of nobody.

When a musician dies, the brass bands get together for the funeral. The

A Joyful Noise

jazz funeral is a tradition that goes way back. When I was a kid, they had the Social and Pleasure Clubs and these different organizations had burial policies. For fifty dollars, you could have a good burial. The band didn't cost you but about twenty dollars at that time; you'd get a casket for fifteen or twenty dollars, and get a couple of carriages and a hearse. The Jolly Bunch, the other clubs, they all had eighteen to twenty kids in the organization. They dressed them in blue suits, white shirts, black ties, and derby hats. The organizations used to dress the same way. I remember once playing three funerals in one day.

When you're going to get the body, you play gospel. It's supposed to be sad. You play sometimes "Just A Closer Walk With Thee" or "Bye and Bye." When you get to the funeral parlor you quiet the band down so as not to disturb the Reverend in there doing his preaching. You stop the band. Sometimes it will be forty-five minutes or an hour. You'll be waiting in that hot sun for the preacher to finish. When we see the body hit the door of the funeral parlor, or the house, or wherever the body is laid out, we strike up a beautiful funeral dirge, maybe "Westlawn," or one of my other favorites. Then we go several blocks down the street. If we're not going to the funeral parlor, we might turn the body loose after five or six blocks, and then on the way back we play a good jazz, something like "Didn't He Ramble," or if he was one of the boys who liked Second Line, Milton (Batiste) might play, "The New Second Line," something like that. Usually when the funeral is going off, we pick up "Saints" if he was somebody we didn't know. But if we knew him and knew he wanted a good time, we might play something else like "Didn't He Ramble," and bring the crowd back.

Sometimes a funeral might last six to eight hours. Sometimes the graveyard might close on you and you'd have to bring the body back the next day because if you get there after five o'clock you don't get in. So you bring the body back the next day and bury the body.

For some of the funerals a long time ago, you had to go to the Social and Pleasure Club meeting place, and then you'd bring them to the house and you'd pick up the body. Then you'd bring them to the church and if it was one of the Baptist churches, you'd be there for a couple of hours. Then after you'd leave the church, you'd bring them to the graveyard. After the graveyard you'd go back to

A Celebration of New Orleans Music

Paul Barbarin funeral   194/10   1969

the clubhouse with the organization, and sometimes you'd be out there six to eight hours. Now, after two to three hours everything is over. The times have changed. The preacher doesn't stay as long. At the Catholic churches, the priest makes his regular service and if the deceased was a member of the church, the priest says some nice words about him. Then we go on... but if the graveyard's too far, we don't go now.

At the Paul Barbarin funeral there were so many people you couldn't even see the wall. You couldn't even see where you were walking. Kid Howard's funeral, as far as you could look, you could see people. I think Paul Barbarin and Alphonse Picou had two of the biggest funerals.

At the funerals nowadays you may see forty or fifty musicians playing. If a musician dies, we invite all the musicians to come out. It hasn't always been that way, but it's been like that for about the last twenty-five years.

Anything can happen at a jazz funeral. Somebody might get shot, and you bury them in the next few days. I've seen people at the bar the deceased bummed at, they might have a big red bean dinner, a big party after the funeral. Usually, after the funeral, they have a certain house they go to and eat and drink. But if it's one of the good-time boys, they're going to ball for a while.

From my understanding, Storyville started at Rampart Street. It was a red light district from Claiborne to Rampart and from St. Louis to Iberville. They had about six or eight clubs with music every night. Musicians could make a living just playing there. They had the jitney dances going on in Storyville. A jitney dance meant a dime a dance. If a fellow wanted to dance with a particular girl, he might buy a hundred tickets and dance with her all night long. As long as she's dancing with him and turning those tickets in, she's getting a certain percentage.

When Storyville was closed down, a lot of musicians had to move to other places. King Oliver and Albert Nicholas moved on to Chicago. That's where the name Dixieland jazz came from. People in Chicago would ask where that music came from and they'd say, "Why, that's Dixieland music from New Orleans." That's how it was named.

I always kept a job; even in the Depression I was playing at the Popeye on Decatur Street. Decatur Street was bigger than Bourbon Street at one time.

A Celebration of New Orleans Music

Paul Barbarin funeral   190/17A   1969

Parade celebrating the reopening of Audubon Park pool (integrated)   254/12   1969

A Celebration of New Orleans Music

I'd finish at the Popeye and go play at Ma-Ma's Place. Then I'd close there and take my banjo player and go play over at the Kingfish. I'd leave the Kingfish and go the next block to the Rose Bowl. Well, I'd get home at six or seven o'clock in the morning and I'd have had a good night's work.

When I was young, my daddy let me travel with bands to Baton Rouge, Alexandria, Shreveport, and all parts of Louisiana. Then, in the summer when there wasn't any school, I'd go to Texas, Arkansas, Missouri, and I'd get to see these western towns that I'd seen in the movies. I enjoyed that very much. Then in later years, Barry Martin, who helped me make my first recordings, invited me to go to London, and I had the opportunity to play at places I guess I thought I never would go. Since then I've made more than twenty-one European trips. I've been all over, anywhere you can mention. People all over the world like the bands, and they're starting to play this traditional New Orleans music. They buy the records and they come here to learn about it. The younger bands in New Orleans, like the Dirty Dozen (Brass Band) and the Rebirth Brass Band, are adding to the music, but they still are based in the tradition.

George Lewis funeral   173/5A   1969

A Celebration of New Orleans Music

"City of New Orleans"   338/26   1970

Mahalia Jackson at the New Orleans Jazz & Heritage Festival   359/15A   1970

A Celebration of New Orleans Music

Woody Allen with the Preservation Hall Band   361/15   1970

Alice May Victor, New Orleans Jazz & Heritage Festival   362/24A   1970

A Celebration of New Orleans Music

Jr. Walker at the "Soul Bowl" Sugar Bowl Stadium   413/10A   1970

Frank Dorsey funeral   990/36   1973

A Celebration of New Orleans Music

George Lewis funeral   168/7A   1969

Roosevelt Sykes, New Orleans Jazz & Heritage Festival   362/29A   1970

A Celebration of New Orleans Music

Sweet Emma Barrett   365/22A   1970

Ambrose Thibodeaux (First New Orleans Jazz & Heritage Festival)   364/20   1970

Roosevelt Sykes, BB King, Bukka White, George Porter and Professor Longhair, New Orleans Jazz & Heritage Festival   845/34   1973

A Celebration of New Orleans Music

Rahsaan Roland Kirk,
New Orleans Jazz &
Heritage Festival
839/11A   1973

Silas Hogan and Guitar Kelly, New Orleans Jazz & Heritage Festival   708/3   1972

A Celebration of New Orleans Music

Kai Winding, Art Tatum, Dizzy Gillespie and Sonny Stitt at the New Orleans Jazz & Heritage Festival   710/32   1972

Professor Longhair and Snooks Eaglin at the New Orleans Jazz & Heritage Festival   711/18   1972

A Celebration of New Orleans Music

Portia's Restaurant   1972

A JOYFUL NOISE

Gerry Mulligan at the
New Orleans Jazz &
Heritage Festival
838/22   1973

A Celebration of New Orleans Music

Albert King, New Orleans Jazz & Heritage Festival 843/31 1973

Babe Stovall   652/11A   1972

Allison "Tootie" Montana

(Big Chief, Yellow Pocahontas Tribe)

At the practices the Indians act out what they are going to do on the street. The Spy Boy will get out there on the floor to act and perform, and if he's doing anything wrong, the Chief will correct him. One time at practice someone was getting carried away and he was down on the ground, and I told him to get up. That's no Indian dance. That's what they do in the Second Line. They get down on their hands. I didn't want to embarrass him in front of the people, but I pulled him off to the side and said, "If you lay down like that, someone from another tribe will step on you. Your ambition is to stay on your feet and to not turn your back on another Chief."

    In those days long ago there was violence, and if you turned your back, you might get your head chopped off or split. The songs are about the dances and some have special meanings. A song they used to sing a long time ago during my daddy's time was "Sore, Sore, Sore." That was a song that they sang Mardi Gras night before World War II. What it meant was that Carnival was over and they had met some tribe and somebody had got hurt. And if your tribe had put some hurt on another tribe, you came back singing that.

A Joyful Noise

I stick to the tradition. I do it the way my daddy and them used to do it, and my daddy did it the way he saw it when he was a boy. Normally, you start practicing the first Sunday after New Year. Carnival is the next holiday.

When I told my mother I was going to mask Indian, she said, "Boy, you're crazy." She knew what it was about. She didn't want me to mask. I have a medal, a scapular in my wallet that my mother would come around and pin on my costume every Carnival. My mother was a strict Catholic and she knew how it used to be. A Carnival hasn't passed since I started masking that my mother wouldn't call that night to see if I was all right. Then she could go to bed.

In my daddy's time you got your name not by your costume, but how bad you were, how violent. They used to fight. All of the tribes had their own location in the neighborhood where they practiced and they would plot and plan against each other. When one tribe meets another, and that Big Chief can make me kneel down, then that's a disgrace. He tells me, "Hum Bah." That means get on your knees. And I say, "No Hum Bah." Now, who's going to get on their knees and bow to another man? And when you didn't do it, that's when the fighting came out. In those days they used to mask with beautiful silk capes, and when they'd come up to you on the street, they'd be covered up and when they'd open that cape a gun would be in their hands. And they'd get away with that because in those days the police didn't have any radio communication in their cars. If there was a misunderstanding they'd have to go back to the station. So the Indians had a lot of opportunities for violence with guns and with real hatchets. They'd paint the blades. The Flag Boys would have iron tips that were sharp. With the Flag Boy running like that, you'd better get out of his way because he could run that thing clean through you.

After World War II, Carnival changed and the fighting stopped, but the tension is always there. It's like going to a party where somebody can't handle their drink and they're going to make trouble. It's no different for the Indians on Carnival day, except that it's open to the public and the chances are greater there than if it was an indoor invitation thing. Each tribe has their Second Liners, so you got these different types of people. Today people run to see the Indians. A long time ago people would run away from the Indians. Today they don't fight physically, they fight with their costumes.

My grandmother told me her brother, Becate Batiste, was with the first tribe in the city, the Creole Wild West. Downtown is the Creole neighborhood. The Creole Wild West started in this area, but they moved uptown where there were a lot of apartments. The Chief of the Creole Wild West during my daddy's time was Robert Sam Tillman, Jr., who was known as Brother Timber and had the reputation of being the baddest on Carnival day, not the prettiest. He didn't make no kind of costume. He'd use a lot of ribbon and he didn't care about the design, but when they said Brother Timber was coming, he was really bad. There was a place up around Magnolia and that was like a battleground. The guys from one side of the Canal didn't want the Indians from the other side to cross there. But my daddy, Alfred Montana, crossed it every time to bring the fight there. My daddy had some bad people with him who could shoot a gun pretty quick. They had large tribes, about fifteen, seventeen, eighteen. They'd have Big Chief, Second Chief, Third Chief, Trail Chief, Flag Boys, Spy Boys, and Wildman or Medicine Man. The ladies were called Queens, and they'd have First Queen, Second Queen. They used to have a Spy Girl, who used to run out there with the men. The song "Indian Red" was like a hymn that was sung on Mardi Gras morning. When it's being sung, it's beautiful, the men's and women's voices mixed together.

The tribes are smaller today. I may have six or seven this year, but I used to have the largest tribe in the city. The second year I masked I was Second Chief with the Eighth Ward Hunters. There were thirty-seven of us, the biggest tribe I ever saw hit the street.

The only day you'd see Indians other than Mardi Gras day was St. Joseph's Night and they'd carry lanterns then. They used to go to a certain place where they'd have a ball, a dance for all the Indians, for the different tribes. St. Joseph's Night was like repeating Carnival over again, but just at night. Some of the Indians would put on their costumes early before it got dark. Then about fifteen years ago they started the Super Sunday parades.

I've been masking for more than forty years. I know how to make all the outfits. I can make the skeleton outfit, the baby doll outfit (with black skirts and pink blouses with puffed sleeves, a black mask, a black whip, and black boots).

Mardi Gras day   1556/30   1978

The men with the Baby Dolls would take two pairs of shoes and make one out of them so they'd be twice as long. I masked with the Baby Dolls about twice, and then I masked skeleton about three times before I masked Indian. The skeleton costume was scary and the Indian was pretty. I wish that some of the young black people knew more about it. During my early years they had the Rosebud Social and Pleasure Club—women who used to mask. Even all the gay people used to mask. They dressed in women's clothes, expensive lace and stockings. Men used to mask as women, and there were even women who would mask as men. The masks were made out of screen wire. The Million Dollar Babies were women who had money, ten, twenty, and fifty dollar bills in their stockings.

Carnival was one day when nobody had to wake you up. Every child in the house (there were ten children in ours) would get up early. If you didn't hear an Indian hollering out there, the smell of the donuts my grandmother was making would wake you up. There was potato salad and ham sandwiches and a big pot of chocolate—we called it cocoa—or coffee. There were people coming to the house all day. It was one big hell of a good time. It was a day you hated to see the sun set. It was beautiful. Today they don't know what they're missing.

The Indians used to be out on the street at six o'clock in the morning, but today they're not. They'd parade and they'd have stops like the Second Liners have today. I'd get all the addresses of different people and sometimes we'd have eight or ten different stops at houses and bars, too. They'd have food and drink, wine, beer, whiskey, red beans and rice, whatever you want. And when you'd stop, sometimes your suit would be coming apart and you'd get a needle and thread and they'd help patch you up.

Indians—years ago you could hear them. They used to use spangles. They used to go by the American Can Factory where they made these cans and they had these cutouts from the cans that would be just about the size of a penny. You'd punch a hole in one end and you'd sew them like shields and when you'd walk they made a sound. Today a whole tribe of Indians can walk up on you and you can't hear them. We used to make noise when we walked. Some of them would have bells under their aprons and when they danced all that stuff would be making noise.

A Joyful Noise

When I was a kid the Carnival parade had a sound to it. It had a feeling. When a parade was five or six blocks away, you had that feeling. You could hear the horse steps. Today they have big rubber tires.

During my daddy's time, they didn't practice in barrooms. They'd rent a little house and they didn't have any electricity and they'd hang a little oil lamp on the wall. All of the members would get together and contribute. It didn't cost too much, maybe five, six dollars a month for a small one- or two-room place. Everyone would only have to pay one or two month's rent. The Chief would lock it up when the practice was over and he'd be there to open it when the practice was ready to start. That way you had privacy to plan and plot what you were going to do when you met the next tribe. Then on Carnival day, they were out there spying with binoculars. The Spy Boy was out there in front, but sometimes there were three or four of them. And then you could have as many Flag Boys as you wanted because guys would come and they'd say they wanted to mask with you because they liked flags. You have to have one responsible Flag Boy, one responsible Spy Boy. The rest of the guys who have less experience can follow.

Today they have Indian practices in barrooms, and some are even charging a cover charge, trying to make it into a nightclub event. They have drums and microphones. In the old days, they had nothing but tambourines according to tradition, no beating on cans or bottles or drums.

The Uptown Indians use the beaded designs more and the small rhinestones. The Downtown Indians, like myself, stick more to what they now call sequins, but my daddy called them fish scales. They were real scales back then; sequins are made out of plastic. The scales had changeable colors when the sun hit them. Today I use some beads, but I prefer the big stones over the small ones.

Uptown they use a lot of ribbon. I don't use ribbon. As far as the feathers, the plumes, they were started by Black Benny from Downtown. Black Benny was Chief of the One Hundred and One Indian tribe. He used to mask with my daddy. He was Second Chief with my daddy, when my daddy was Big Chief of the Yellow Pocahontas, which is the tribe I have now. Black Benny came out one year in red loaded with pins and pom-poms. He was pretty in those times. He had short red plumes. And the next year he came out in an identical suit, but with white ones.

A Celebration of New Orleans Music

The Wild Magnolias "Mardi Gras Indian" tribe at the Professor Longhair fire benefit   1122/34   1974

A JOYFUL NOISE

The year after that the Chief of the White Eagles, who used to be my competition Uptown, came out with blue and white plumes. And everybody Uptown has been using plumes ever since.

Plumes are a cover-up. I'd rather use feathers. I used to get turkey feathers. I'd go around to the places that I knew sold chickens and turkeys and I'd talk to the guy and he'd put them up for me.

The headpiece is called the crown and the trails are hooked to the headpiece. The apron is the front, and then a belt hooks onto the apron. On the back of the crown, you can make a double row or a triple. Then there are different wing feathers. This year I'm going to use plume tips. The feathers come from the wings and the plumes come from the tail.

When I used the turkey feathers, I'd have to dye them myself. The turkey feathers are grey and have stripes in them. A lot of guys used them just the way they were. But then when the different-colored feathers started coming out, we started buying them. Feathers have always been my thing. Everybody in my tribe wears feathers. We have a different style of sewing. It's a lot of work. When I'm stringing my feathers, I have to make a loop on each one. When I'm pulling my needle through, I pull it back and loop it and that locks the feather in. Then I wrap them so they stay flexible in the wind. A crown is supposed to work for you. If I'm standing up and the wind is behind me, the crown moves. With the plumes there's less control.

My daddy was a Chief for almost forty years. What started me off was that my daddy had helped these boys in the Eighth Ward to form a gang, and I told him I wanted to mask, too. Carnival was three weeks away. He said, "You want to mask. When? Next year?"

I said, "No, this year." I didn't know what I was doing but I made a little suit. That was 1947 and I've been masking ever since.

I worked as a metal lather. I shaped up houses with wire, with the studs and the metal and whatever. I did the background for the plaster. I built the frame with metal and wire. I shaped arches and other forms. It's like designing my costumes. Any costume, anything I make, I start off with a center line. When you look at my costume, it's straight and balanced. My brother, Edward, he can take

A Celebration of New Orleans Music

Johnny Diggs, Chief of the Wild Tchoupitoulas   2298/3   1984

Mardi Gras Indian with live bird in bonnet
2286/11   1984

Chief "Jolly" George Landry (Wild Tchoupitoulas "Mardi Gras Indian" tribe), Mardi Gras day   1560/4A   1978

a pencil and sit down and draw you. I can't do that, but I can do design. Edward is my Second Chief.

When it comes to creating, God—the man up there—gives that to you, and I thank Him every night for giving me the knowledge to understand and do so much. When it comes to Indian suits, I design and create just about anything with my own ideas. I don't want what I've seen anywhere else.

Over the last ten years, the Mardi Gras Indians have changed a lot. I'm doing it today mostly for the people, for the public. Last year I didn't mask. I took my camera and walked the street looking for the Indians myself. With the cost of living a lot of guys can't afford it. That material is sky-high, and besides, you can hardly find it. I went to the costume place and the small stones that used to be thirty cents a dozen were a dollar eighty cents a dozen and they weren't glass, they were plastic.

My design ideas come strictly out of my head. I sit down and create it. Sometimes it takes weeks, cutting up cardboard, drawing designs, trying to create and get different ideas. I change my costumes every year. There are a lot of people out there who only get ideas from what they see. If I didn't change my costume, somebody might copy it and one of these times we'd be out there on the street alike. I throw them off; they never see the same thing twice. The next year I'm going to jump ahead. When you've been doing this as long as I have, the past keeps coming to my mind and blocking what I want to do for now. It's confusing. Sometimes I create a design and my wife, who's very familiar with my designs, will come in and say, "You're not going to use that."

I'll say, "Why, what's the matter?"

"Don't you remember you had that one year?"

I'll say, "You know, I thought I had something like that." Now, that's no good. I've got to tear it up and start from scratch again. My brother makes his costume the same way.

I've never used the same design. You can look at my pictures. Some of the stuff I've made I'd like to use again. The reason I don't want to go back to it is that since then so many other guys have used it.

I make my costumes very different than a lot of people because what you

see on me is nothing that you'll ever see anywhere else. I see it like a picture, and I draw it, and I better draw it fast because sometimes I close my eyes and see pictures in my head. And at another time when I want the picture to come back, it won't come back the same way. So, I sit at the table at night when it's quiet. The picture starts coming into my head and I grab a pencil and sketch it right quick when it's there. It comes just like a cloud, floats right through my mind and goes on. If I don't bring it into reality, then it's lost.

Dizzy Gillespie and Bongo Joe at the New Orleans Jazz & Heritage Festival   540/26   1971

A Celebration of New Orleans Music

Lee Dorsey at work 1195/11 1974

BB King, New Orleans Jazz & Heritage Festival   850/30A   1973

A Celebration of New Orleans Music

Sister Gertrude Morgan and Allan Jaffe at the New Orleans Jazz & Heritage Festival   851/19   1973

Professor Longhair at
New Orleans
Parish Prison
943/35 1973

A Celebration of New Orleans Music

Como Fife and Drum Corps   856/25A   1973

Herbie Hancock, New Orleans Jazz & Heritage Festival
1128/6A   1974

A Joyful Noise

Howlin' Wolf, New Orleans Jazz & Heritage Festival
856/10A   1973

Stevie Wonder jamming with the Meters, New Orleans Jazz & Heritage Festival   836/16   1973

A Celebration of New Orleans Music

Kid Thomas Valentine and Algiers Stompers, New Orleans Jazz & Heritage Festival   1131/34   1974

Lightnin' Hopkins, New Orleans Jazz & Heritage Festival   1136/12A   1974

Johnny "Kool" Stephenson

(Member, Scene Boosters Marching Club,
Money Wasters Marching Club, Wild Magnolias Indian Tribe)

The economy has caused a lot of changes. When people have problems financially, they tend to go the cheaper way. They try to make the cheaper way look as good as the expensive way, but it doesn't turn out that way in all cases. We try to save as much money as we can, but it really doesn't make sense. If you want to be number one, as they say, you've got to spend the money to be number one. We spend money and we spend big money. Sometimes you can get lucky, and come into a situation where the group is so strong it doesn't matter how you look or what you do, the name carries it. We try to keep things going traditionally as much as we can.

There's a fairly new group called the Buck Jumpers and they came out storming. They were really ringing it. Everybody was excited over them and then all of a sudden they were down in a short period of time to the point where they didn't have many members left. I don't know why.

I'm fortunate enough to be in the top organizations. As far as marching, the Boosters are recognized as one of the top organizations, and as Indians, I think the Wild Magnolias are one of the top. They are well-known. I'll put it to

A Joyful Noise

you this way: I've been marching in parades for seventeen years and over those seventeen years I've been a Booster. I've been with a group called the Scene Highlighters. That was my original group. Then I went to the Scene Boosters and from there on to the Money Wasters.

The city basically wants to stop it, but they can't stop it because it's a traditional thing. But, they put such a tax on you now that it is really hard to parade.

For the Boosters you might need four divisions with bands and we've averaged as high as $1,600 for the permit and the police. That's the highest it's ever been. The lowest, back in 1972 I think, was about $260. Now that's a lot of years in between, but still $1,600 is a lot of money.

My knowledge of Second Line parades goes back into the late 1800s. It all had to do with funerals, benevolent associations, and celebrations. We still do it, but we do it a little bit different. We don't just do it for funerals. We have an annual parade. And if somebody dies and they were a Second Line follower, and if their relatives want this, then we have it. Sometimes the family will pay for the band. Sometimes the Club will pay for the band. Then if the guy was well-known in the organization, it's free. The bands will participate in a free situation, like with James Black, for instance. He was a well-known musician, the most recent that has passed. They really gave him a good sendoff, especially the night of the wake, a jazz set you would not have believed. They played after the wake at a nightclub around the corner. Everybody gathered there, and they had forty or fifty musicians taking turns playing, just a jam session, but they really got it on.

I've seen pictures of parades from as early as 1855, old photographs of wagons and long dresses and the guys with black tuxedos on. They were parading. It might have started earlier than that, I just don't know, but when you really think about it, that's Second Line. If you think about how people paraded in the street before, it's not much different.

I got involved when I was about fifteen years old. What happened was that there was this old fellow they called Ghost, and Ghost was in the Young Men Olympians. He used to take the kids out of the neighborhood to the parades. I was younger, maybe ten years old, when I first started going, but I wasn't involved on a parading basis as far as being a member. Ghost used to take us there and get us in a little group on the sidewalk. They'd be on the street and we'd be on the sidewalk and we'd be parading alongside the band having fun, just dancing. So you see what he was actually doing was preparing us for this, but we didn't look at it that way. We were just going out there and doing what we wanted to do. So Ghost died, and when he died, all the little guys went their own way.

After I came home from the Vietnam War—I had been injured in the war and I didn't think I could do it—I went to a Second Line parade and I still could boogie. So I said, I'm going to join. And I decided I wanted to join a group with young men my age that I knew. They were past schoolmates of mine and we decided we were going to call it the Scene Highlighters. That was a kicker. It was wild. Everybody was shocked. Here came these young men. All of the other clubs at that time consisted of older people. But when we hit the streets, we had young ideas, new ideas. We lasted about ten years. We started in 1971 and broke up in 1981. I left them in 1978. After that I joined the Scene Boosters and I've been with them up until a year ago. They were an older club in the sense that the guys in that club had paraded with other clubs before. They had retired or stopped from the other groups. The Scene Boosters were a help to us as the Scene Highlighters. They backed us up. We appreciated that, but we wanted something different. Traditionally, it was umbrellas; that was it. The Uptown clubs had umbrellas, and the Downtown clubs had baskets. When we started, we brought baskets out, the Scene Highlighters did. The Scene Boosters brought them out after we did.

The first year one of the groups had umbrellas and baskets. One of the groups had umbrellas and walking canes. One of the groups had fans and baskets. Feathers started about fifteen years ago. Before then all they had were ribbon fans or a marabou or papier-maché, anything they thought they could do. You see, those were economical times. Plumes were so expensive. One plume cost seventy-eight dollars. A plume fan takes fifteen to twenty plumes. You add that up, and you're talking about some serious money just for one fan. We did it as the Scene Highlighters because we wanted to spend the money. We knew what it was going to take to do it. We used ostrich plumes. They average from twenty-four inches to thirty-five inches in length. The ones we got came from Australia.

I also use plumes when I mask as an Indian. This is my fifth year. I masked

Scene Boosters Social & Pleasure Club annual parade   2273/10A   1983

Indian before, twenty years ago, but I'd mask one year and I wouldn't mask for three or four years. It was a spur of the moment thing for me. If I felt like I wanted to do it, I had the equipment to do it. I sat down and I sewed and I sewed and when Carnival time came, I hit the streets. But at that time I was doing what they called "running as a renegade." I didn't belong to any gang.

Then I had the opportunity to meet Jake, the Chief of the White Eagles. He told me that I shouldn't run renegade because I had a pretty good thing as far as the Indians go. He said I was doing it pretty good and that I should get into it on a more regular basis. So for about two more years I stayed out and I just sewed and kept myself kind of undercover. Then I made my move, but I didn't join Jake's gang, the White Eagles, because they are a Downtown gang. I'm an Uptown man, I come from Uptown, so I want to be in an Uptown gang. Bo Dollis, with the Wild Magnolias, is the chief of an Uptown gang, and he's a friend. I told him I wanted to be in the Wild Magnolias and he said, "Fine."

The Wild Magnolias have been on the streets since 1889. I don't know for sure. It may have been before that. That's what I learned from the oldest living Chief. I met him through a black history show at a junior high school here. He happened to be a speaker there. During the break time, I had a chance to talk to him. He explained to me how the Indians were helpful to the blacks, and how we broke away from slavery and went to the Indians, and how the Indians taught us so many things about their culture. And for some reason or other—why and how I don't know—we became Indians ourselves later, only for Mardi Gras. At celebration time, everybody had a different thing they wanted to do and we made our costumes to signify Mardi Gras Indians.

To me, all of it is a togetherness-type of thing. They all are groups. The Indians are a group and the Second Liners are a group. They do things in church, they sing and they dance and feel the spirit. That's what church is all about. They praise the Lord.

With Mardi Gras Indians we do the same thing in a sense. We sing, we party, we dance, and we even have our prayer. We praise our past Indians when we sing "Indian Red." It's like an Indian national anthem.

When we start out on Mardi Gras morning, our Chief will stand in the

A JOYFUL NOISE

middle of the street and he'll start singing "Indian Red." All Indian gangs do it a little bit different, but it still boils down to the same thing. He's going to sing this song and each of his Indian members will approach him and give a signal and he'll send us on our way while the song is still being sung. And as we go through the crowd, it's like he's saying, "Bye, but good luck. It's going to be all right." It's just a prayer for our protection. That's the way I learned it. It's to take care of you. It's to praise the past Indians.

When any Indian leaves this world, we go to his wake or funeral and we sing "Indian Red." It's a tribute to a good Indian. It's a tribute to past Indians, and to us on that Mardi Gras morning because that's our big day.

We have fifteen members in the Wild Magnolias. Everyone has a different role unless you're running double.

You've got a Wild Man, Medicine Man, Spy Boy, First Flag, Second Flag, Gang Flag, Council Chief, Second Chief, Big Chief, Witch Doctor. Medicine Man is just simply that, the medicine man, and he dresses totally differently. The Witch Doctor stays with the Big Chief. He protects the Chief. We all protect him, but the Witch Doctor is at the front of the group destroying all of the evil. He usually does a little dance. He's got some kind of shaker. The Wild Man stays in the back with the Chief, but he can run all over. He's a runner when the Chief wants to get a signal to the front and can't get it. He will tell the Wild Man verbally and the Wild Man will move to the front and tell them what's going on.

I am a Gang Flag carrier. In my position, I'm the fourth man in front of the Chief. I control the gang. My flag says "Wild Magnolias" on one side and on the other side it says "Flag Boy." It's a tradition to have a Gang Flag, but some gangs aren't big enough to have one. Some just have a Flag Boy. Our Flag Boy is a runner in front of me. He plays with me. What I mean by that is that we run around and dance. I'm waving my flag all over and he's got his flag. When we meet an Indian gang that's coming, he'll come to me and we'll get side by side and we'll put the two flags down like a gate. And they can't come through that gate unless we open it. We don't touch each other. We're not supposed to touch each other. That's the sign of trouble. There might be a fight or even killing. In my time, I've been lucky. I came into it when the fighting and stuff was slacking off. Now it does

A Celebration of New Orleans Music

Chief Bo Dollis (Wild Magnolias "Mardi Gras Indian" tribe) at Hercules' funeral   1720/17   1979

happen. We have had guys come out there with knives and guns, Indians attacking each other. I don't remember any outsiders attacking an Indian. It comes from the competition. For some, it's a jealousy thing.

You sew a good nine months of the year and you try to hide your stuff, but it gets out one way or another. I know a guy who will actually come to your house and wait for you.

Some people respond negatively to the presence of white people for that reason. When a white man comes into the neighborhood and he photographs and he videos and tapes and talks and gets good stuff out of the community that no black man has gotten, or even tried to get, some people are going to say, "Yeah, Mike Smith, he came here and then wrote a book. He did this in the black community." Hey man, look, if you don't do it, who in the hell is going to do it? For me, it is an uplifting thing for the black community. It brings us closer together.

I've heard of Indians in the churches. The Indians I deal with are not members of the Spiritualist churches, but they are members of churches. They all go to church, Baptist, Catholic, or whatever. A lot of Indians don't go to church, but most of the Second Liners do. The Second Line came from church. They played funerals or celebrations or church anniversaries. The bands still march in the church and play. They play hymns and things like that in church. But once you're out of the church, you can kick off into any kind of jumping music because you're celebrating.

When I left the Scene Highlighters in 1979 after the Ball and joined the Scene Boosters in 1980, I was voted Vice President of the Boosters for three years. Then I was voted President. We were an organization that got lucky. We did a lot of traveling, performing. We performed at the White House. We performed in Chicago, California, at different folk festivals. A few times while we were on these trips we were hired by different nightclubs to perform with other bands. It wasn't a parading thing. They would just take two or three guys and the band on the stage and we'd be Second Line dancing. It's the same thing, but it's just not on the streets.

When we went to Washington, D.C., we were on Pennsylvania Avenue walking toward the entry on the side of the White House. The little badge they gave us told us where we had to go to get in. I don't know why, but the band started playing and we started dancing. Here that's normal, but there the people looked at us like we were crazy. The Secret Service came running out there with the dogs and all this sort of stuff. They made us stop playing and they questioned us. They had us all line up and sort of searched us, but then the guy who was in charge came and we told who we were and about tradition and about what we do. The man in charge apologized. He was real nice. They understood and they let us play. And we went along and we played on the sidewalk. That was in 1973. We played on a little stage in back of the White House and they gave us little medals.

Some band members are part of the clubs, but the bands play for all the different clubs. Some of the bands may have a hundred members, but maybe out of that you've got five people that belong to a club. Each of the bands have eight to ten members. They have a horn section with trumpet and trombone and the bass horn, drum section, snare drum, bass drum. Sometimes alto and tenor saxophone. In a more traditional band, such as the Young Tuxedos, you might have clarinets, a banjo, guitar. There are about fifteen different marching bands in the city now. They don't all play on the streets. There's the Olympia Brass Band, Chosen Few, Pin Stripe, Majestic, All Star, Rebirth, Young Tuxedos, Algiers, and the Doc Paulin Brass Band. Doc Paulin is an old musician who has brought back the tradition with young people to keep his band going.

What we do in clubs is raise money to put something into the community. When I say "we" I mean the Scene Boosters and the Money Wasters clubs. We give block parties, dances, and we make a little money. We'll sell beer or hot dogs, things like that, but there are times we don't do any of those things. We'll give parties for the kids, for instance. What the Boosters did was get lights in the park. For a lot of years Shakespeare Park didn't have any lights in it, and there was a lot of drug dealing and rapes and fights and murders. Now, when you pass there at night, it looks like daytime because of what the Boosters did.

We try to have a positive impact on the community. That's what we want. All clubs try to do this, but sometimes they get a little carried away with one thing. Sometimes all they want to do is parade.

Gate Johnson funeral, Avenue Steppers and Scene Boosters Social & Pleasure Club   2215/7A   1983

The Indians are totally different. With the Indians it's a "self" thing. You do it for you. You work hard all year making this costume to show off on Mardi Gras day. And if it's not pretty, you know it when you walk out that door.

It builds self-esteem. You want to let Indians across the street know, *I'm ready. C'mon, I'm ready. You come show me your suit and I'm going to show you mine.* We are going to find out who's the baddest, that kind of a thing. Fortunately, with the Wild Magnolias, we're such a popular group, we get a lot of shows to do. We do a lot of traveling, making pretty decent money, getting money back from the costumes that we've worked and spent so much money for. We spend thousands of dollars to make a costume, maybe $2,500 for a costume, a certain costume. Not all Indians dress the same way, or put the same amount of money into their work. There are what they call sequined Indian suits. That's a cheaper way of doing it than with beads, much cheaper. You see, we work with beads and stones. I estimate the value of my suit to be about $6,000. If I were to sell it as a full made-up suit, it would be worth $10,000. There's value in time, labor, and the materials put into it. When I travel with my suit, I put down on the insurance for the plane $20,000. I want them to understand what it's worth. That's probably closer to the real value when you consider the time to make it.

You rearrange your patches every year. You arrange them and you make more, or you tear down certain patches and rearrange them. They are supposed to tell a story. Most Indians that I deal with—Wild Magnolias, Creole Wild West, Black Eagles—Uptown Mardi Gras Indians, we basically mask the same way. What I mean by that is beads, stones, plumes, things like that. The front of our suits from the neck on down to the ankle tells a story. This man, Indian Nat, he always told a story in his suit. It was real easy to read just by looking at it. It depended on what he wanted to say. I couldn't say what his story was, but it would be, say, an Indian and a maiden up here, then perhaps lower down would be a family of Indians, and then below it might be the cavalry, and then below that might be a wagon train, like in a cartoon. Each little section told something. He had a way of doing it that told a straight-out story that you could read as plain as day. You wouldn't have to know it, you could see it.

The Downtown Indians have a totally different approach. Downtown Indians

wear sequins, a lot of glued-on patches, mirrors, pearls, things like that. It's more abstract. They glue instead of sewing. It's still a lot of work. But for my suit, I figure if I sew it down right it ain't going nowhere. After about two or three hours of running and clowning and playing, you're sweating, your suit is soaking wet, the pearls and that glue are not going to do as they're told, and normally it works out that way. It doesn't mean that all of it will come off, but some of it will.

When the Council started two years ago, they estimated twenty-seven Indian gangs and now they say thirty-three. So, who knows? It goes up and down. It goes with the economy more or less because if you don't have money, you don't hit the streets. It's that simple. That's the reality you have to face. I've got bills to pay. I've got a car note, a house note. I've got to put food in the house. So, you make a choice. Either you don't pay the bills and be Indian or don't be Indian and pay the bills.

My baby boy has masked Indian with me before and he's going to mask with me again this year. My wife helps with the sewing. The whole family does something. It's a family-involved thing. Both the Indians and the Second Line parades are family-oriented.

I'm forty-one years old now. I'm a disabled vet, ex-Marine. I'm saying that because I'm a proud Marine. The New Orleans Police Department gave me the nickname Johnny Kool when I was about ten years old. I was sitting on a porch in the projects and when the police came we used to run, but I didn't run. And they had the loud speakers on top of the car and one policeman said to the other, "Oh, he wants to be cool. He doesn't want to run." So they got out of the car and approached me and talked to me. They asked me who I was. I told them my name was Johnny. "Oh, this is cool Johnny." So I turned it around from cool Johnny to Johnny Kool. That's the way it went and I've been called that from that day forward.

A Celebration of New Orleans Music

Irma Thomas, New Orleans Jazz & Heritage Festival   1315/17   1975

Earl King, New Orleans Jazz & Heritage Festival   1306/4   1975

A Celebration of New Orleans Music

James Booker, New Orleans Jazz & Heritage Festival   1305/26A   1975

Professor Longhair, New Orleans Jazz & Heritage Festival   1445/25   1977

A Celebration of New Orleans Music

Hands of Professor Longhair, December 19, 1977   1538/36   1977

Monk Boudreaux, Chief of the Golden Eagles
1212/17   1974

Archbishop B.S. Johnson, Eternal Life Christian Spiritual Church   1971

A Celebration of New Orleans Music

Cajun Bar-B-Que   1580/16   1978

"Let the truth be told": Desire project, New Orleans   1976

A Celebration of New Orleans Music

Bus stop at Washington and Clairborne Streets   1976

Emmanuel Sayles on banjo, New Orleans Jazz & Heritage Festival   1142/29A   1974

A Celebration of New Orleans Music

Aaron Neville, New Orleans Jazz & Heritage Festival   1453/34   1977

A JOYFUL NOISE

Bobby Bland, New Orleans Jazz & Heritage Festival   1449/12A   1977

A Celebration of New Orleans Music

The Dixie Cups, New Orleans Jazz & Heritage Festival   1460/10   1977

"Gatemouth" Brown, New Orleans Jazz & Heritage Festival   1370/27A   1976

A Celebration of New Orleans Music

Allen Toussaint, New Orleans Jazz & Heritage Festival   1462/14A   1977

Lee Dorsey, New Orleans Jazz & Heritage Festival   1462/20A   1977

A Celebration of New Orleans Music

Snooks Eaglin, New Orleans Jazz & Heritage Festival   1448/35   1977

Lu and Danny Barker with Tuts Washington at Tipitina's   1575/31   1978

A Celebration of New Orleans Music

Professor Longhair at Tipitina's   1579/36   1978

James Booker, New Orleans Jazz & Heritage Festival   1608/12A   1978

Sylvester Francis

(Member, Gentlemen of Leisure Social and Pleasure Club/Community Documentarian)

I was in a Social and Pleasure Club about eight or nine years ago and after the first year we paraded, we had nothing to do but talk about the parades. So, I went out and bought a camera, so the next time I paraded I could take some pictures. In the meantime, they had a couple of jazz funerals and different things happened. And from there I just kept doing it. That's how I started, by shooting it, and as I shot it, people would say, "Oooh man, that's something nice."

After I really got into it and started talking to people, I was surprised that nobody was really keeping any kind of record. Even a lot of the old-time Indians don't have pictures of themselves. It amazed me that these guys masked twenty years ago, or fifteen years ago, and they've got the memory and that's all.

The history was passed on, but it was never kept. Today some of the clubs are trying to keep their own history. The Jolly Bunch, for example, is one of the oldest clubs. They can tell you about it, but as far as having something to prove what they say, they don't. They don't have many photographs. There is more interest today in saving things than there was ten years ago.

The participation in the clubs is declining, but money is the biggest problem

Avenue Steppers Marching Club annual banner blessing parade   2101/23   1982

now. Some of the guys who are not parading now are sending their children out to keep it going.

I met Mike Smith on the street one day. We bumped into one another and he told me he'd like to see my stuff. So when I did show it to him, half of the stuff was wrong and he just gave me advice on what to correct. I had the wrong splicing machine. I was using the wrong color film. As he told me what to do, I started changing and I wound up buying a little better equipment as I went along. When I'm able I'll buy some more better equipment. Just keep stepping up.

We are in two different fields. Mike has been doing it much longer than me. I shoot Super-8 movies. Our documents are not really documentaries. We are just saving the raw footage to make documentaries. But he is documenting as he goes along. He's bringing it out.

People in the black community feel it's more important for you to know what happened a long time ago. The community is ready to be documented and they should be.

I'm a member of the Gentlemen of Leisure Social and Pleasure Club. Gentlemen of Leisure, that's a Seventh Ward Club. The city of New Orleans is divided into wards. It's a parade club. We save our money to parade once a year like all the rest of the clubs.

In our club we have to go by our by-laws and our club, being small, has to stick to the basics. We can help our members. If we don't have enough money, we'll have a small function to raise the money.

One story I heard was that a long time ago the whites didn't want the blacks in the Mardi Gras parade. So the blacks took the off-season and made their own little parades. This grew to be known as the Second Line parades with the Social and Pleasure Clubs.

In some of my films you can see a five-year difference with the dress. In some clubs, you can see that they had four, five, six hundred dollars worth of clothes on. Right now, they've cut down to a hundred-and-a-half to two hundred dollars. One year the Scene Boosters wore leather suits. Two years later they came out with shirts and pants on. It's a big difference. You can see how the parades have taken a turn moneywise.

The bands cost more. The permits cost more. The clubs have to raise all the money.

The whole family is involved in the parade in the street. And the whole family has to sacrifice the whole year.

None of the Second Line parades get any outside funding. All the clubs through the whole year have to give functions to raise the money. The clubs support each other. During the parades, the other clubs might sell beer and soft drinks to help them parade. We give card games, suppers, dances, parties, discos. All of this has to happen all year just for one parade. Most clubs try to do something every other week, even if it's just something among themselves. Then when you get down to the wire, you've got to tax yourself. Like us—we have to give fifteen dollars every two weeks. Then when we get to that last month, we have to tax ourselves a hundred or hundred-fifty dollars more. So some of the clubs can't parade every year.

A Celebration of New Orleans Music

Fats Domino on the President, New Orleans Jazz & Heritage Festival   1931/37   1981

Clifton Chenier, New Orleans Jazz & Heritage Festival   1961/6A   1981

A Celebration of New Orleans Music

Paul Barnes funeral   1837/32   1981

Doug Kershaw, New Orleans Jazz & Heritage Festival   1616/J1-5   1978

A Celebration of New Orleans Music

Huey Smith at Tipitina's   1684/4   1979

A Joyful Noise

Dave Bartholomew at benefit for WWOZ 90.7 FM for Community Radio   2068/31A   1982

A Celebration of New Orleans Music

Dr. John "The Night Tripper" at Tipitina's   2036/11A   1982

A JOYFUL NOISE

Chuck Berry at the
New Orleans Jazz &
Heritage Festival
2070/28 1982

A Celebration of New Orleans Music

William Walker and the Mighty Chariots, New Orleans Jazz & Heritage Festival   1742/29   1979

End of Mt. Moriah Missionary Baptist Church's annual parade   1755/25   1979

A Celebration of New Orleans Music

The Zion Harmonizers
at the New Orleans
Jazz & Heritage Festival
2078/19   1982

Etta James, New Orleans Jazz & Heritage Festival   1743/29A   1979

A Celebration of New Orleans Music

Professor Longhair, New Orleans Jazz & Heritage Festival   1751/5A   1979

James Booker signs his album, New Orleans Jazz & Heritage Festival   1742/22   1979

126

A Celebration of New Orleans Music

Roger Lewis, Red Tyler, Lee Allen and Tommy Ridgley jamming at a benefit for WWOZ 90.7 FM for Community Radio   2068/10   1982

Professor Longhair and
Mrs. Henry Roeland
Byrd at home
1763/4A 1979

A Celebration of New Orleans Music

Mr. and Mrs. Henry Roeland Byrd at Civil Defense (Special Forces 714) Meeting   1763/23A   1979

Chief Larry Bannock (Golden Star Hunters "Mardi Gras Indian" tribe)   2124/3   1983

A Celebration of New Orleans Music

Civil Defense group (Special Forces 714) at annual church celebration   1768/9   1979

The Neville Brothers plus Ivan (Aaron's son) at the Patio Lounge   1831/16   1980

A Celebration of New Orleans Music

Fats Houston funeral   1920/26A   1981

"Big Linda" at Dorothy's Medallion Lounge with George Porter and David Lastie band   1901/21   1981

A Celebration of New Orleans Music

Ernie K-Doe's birthday party at Winny's Lounge   1923/13   1981

Betty Carter, New Orleans Jazz & Heritage Festival   1955/9A   1981

Larry Bannock

(Chief, Golden Star Hunters Mardi Gras Indian Tribe)

Indians don't have any problem with people taking pictures. The only problem comes in the *way* people take pictures. A lot of times they ask you to get in the right position. When you're meeting your tribe, you can't stop and pose. A lot of people don't have the courtesy to ask your name. So it got to the point that Indians just closed up when people came in with cameras.

Very few people have a chance to see what's really going on. Mike Smith was one of the first. At least, a lot of people trust him. He's the only one that can go certain places now, to see one of these costumes hooked up.

A lot of people come to New Orleans to take pictures and to get information and they tell you they're going to send you pictures or write you about what they did, but you never hear from them again. So it took Mike a long time to build up trust because it's kind of hard to see a white boy come around all of a sudden taking pictures and interested in the culture. For a long time this was kept mainly in the black neighborhoods. They wouldn't let anybody in. They wouldn't talk to anybody.

Very few get the close-up information, about what people wear what mask,

Norman Bell (2nd Chief, Wild Tchoupitoulas "Mardi Gras Indian" tribe) birthday party at the Patio Lounge   1669/28A   1979

A Celebration of New Orleans Music

Mardi Gras Indian   2446/34   1986

Mardi Gras Indian, "Super Sunday"
parade   2880/21   1989

A Joyful Noise

what the different signals mean, what the difference is between Uptown and Downtown Indians, what Indians sewed and what Indians played. Uptown Indians wear two suits, Downtown Indians wear one. They wear creative designs, and Uptown Indians wear repeated designs.

A lot of white photographers, you only see them at Jazz Fest. Mike is around all year. Just about everybody has his phone number and everybody knows him. That makes a big difference. Mike gives away a lot, maybe too much. He's the only photographer I know who will come up and talk to you and even help you any way he can—let you know about grants, let you know about people coming to town. He goes beyond his duty. He takes interest when a lot of blacks do not.

The Indians started to become public in the 1980s. Mike made an effort to talk to everyone so that they knew what he was going to do. The Indian thing is dying, and he's trying to help preserve it.

When I first started in 1972, all you needed was four patches, and now you need twenty-some patches to make a costume.

Mike didn't come in and just bullshit with you and play with your mind. Whatever he told you, it was fact. He didn't try to manipulate or use you.

There was a guy who came here from France. He stayed a long time. Every Sunday night you'd see him at practice with a handkerchief or flag around his head like he wanted to be one of us. But after he wrote the book he disappeared. That's natural, but the way he wrote the book, he didn't really tell what the Indian story was about.

People ask, "Why do you mask Indian?" That's the big question.

It's because when the blacks were slaves they would run away and the Indians were the only people who accepted them. They didn't ask a whole lot of questions. They didn't inquire.

But now people are beginning to ask questions. For a long time all you heard about in New Orleans was Rex and Zulu and now people are beginning to see that the Indians have been out there for a long time, and they're respected. When you go places now and you say Mardi Gras Indians, people know something about them. This is a grass-roots thing, a neighborhood thing. It takes a lot of people working together to make it *come* together. To make an Indian suit you need the help of a lot of people. My Indian suit—I sew it, but there are a lot of outside people who contribute. Mike will give me a picture, or a guy I know named Jim will take my picture and blow it up and put it in an art gallery.

People just don't understand where a white photographer's coming from because when a man comes to you with a whole lot of promises, you can bet he's phony. Like Mike will tell you, people will come to town and they say they'll write you or send you a picture.

There was an incident one time when this reporter came to New Orleans to interview the Indians. Somehow an incident broke out and she got hurt. A lot of people got the wrong impression about Indians. But there is a way you're supposed to come up to a Chief. Carnival day you don't just go up to Rex and start taking pictures and talking to him. There's a chain of command. You've got to go through the Spy Boy, Gang Flagman, and tell them what you want to do and ask permission. It takes some time to get there with the cameras and get set up and this and that. And you only have so much time. It's kind of hard walking from Downtown to Uptown.

Now, people will call you up and ask you if they can come over. That way everybody starts to respect you.

National Geographic was the first group to really show concern. When they came in they talked to a lot of different people, old Indians, young Indians, anybody who had something to contribute. It got to the point where they were even calling long distance to talk to people.

People don't mind working with something when they feel they are a part of it. A lot of times people come here during the Jazz Fest. There are photographers here from all over the world and they insult you. Often they don't find out who they're taking a picture of. The just take a picture of an "Indian." Next thing you know they have the wrong name under the picture.

In this year's program of the Jazz Fest (1988) there was an ad for Ripley's Believe It or Not that had a picture of an Indian. It's a Golden Star suit and they identify it as Chief of the Wild Magnolias. Well, this picture was taken back in 1974, the year I got shot. That was the suit that caused the shooting.

What happened was that the two gangs were split. The Golden Star tribe

A JOYFUL NOISE

was up there and the Red, White, and Blue was over there. Well, the two Spy Boys started playing, with the Second Liners instigating it. I was prettier than the other Spy Boy. And someone kept ribbing him and the next thing you knew things got out of hand. That's the purpose of the Spy Boy—to keep things from getting out of control. That was my first year running as First Spy and after I got that bullet I learned something about how to play my position.

People come in and take pictures and then your picture is in a magazine with someone else's name. We are beginning to deal with the issue of somebody's taking pictures of you and selling them, when they don't even have the respect to get the right name. Mike never does that. He takes the interest to find out, while some white photographers take pictures of you and they go click, click, click, click. Some black photographers come in with that "Brother" shit and a whole lot of pipe dreams. He's going to show you how the pictures are going to help you, but he won't even give you his phone number. Sometimes when people come to take pictures of me, I just fold up. You don't want anybody taking your picture that won't pay you respect. It doesn't matter, white or black. It's the attitude of the photographer that's important.

The attitude and the respect. A lot of blacks that take pictures are amateurs. Sometimes they want to take your picture with their wife and child. But when a professional takes your picture, sometimes it's best to set up, or let you know it's going to happen. But you have to deal with it when it comes down.

Respect is what it's all about. It doesn't make sense going through all this sewing, and fingers blistering and bleeding, if it can't be shown. You know, because of Mike Smith talking to the right people and bringing them around, this is now considered artwork. I have a suit at the St. Louis Art Museum going around the world for two years. After two years, whatever happens to it happens. But if Mike wouldn't have taken his time . . . and believe it or not, Mike opened the doors for a lot of photographers. Still, very few acknowledge who got them in. If Mike hadn't made the phone call and talked to you and said, "This person is okay. He won't mess you around," then it wouldn't happen.

My tribe is the Golden Star Hunters, Sixteenth and Seventeenth Wards. Basically, every black section of New Orleans has an Indian gang. There's only

A Celebration of New Orleans Music

Monk Boudreaux, Chief
of the Golden Eagles
(First New Orleans Jazz
& Heritage Festival)
363/14A   1970

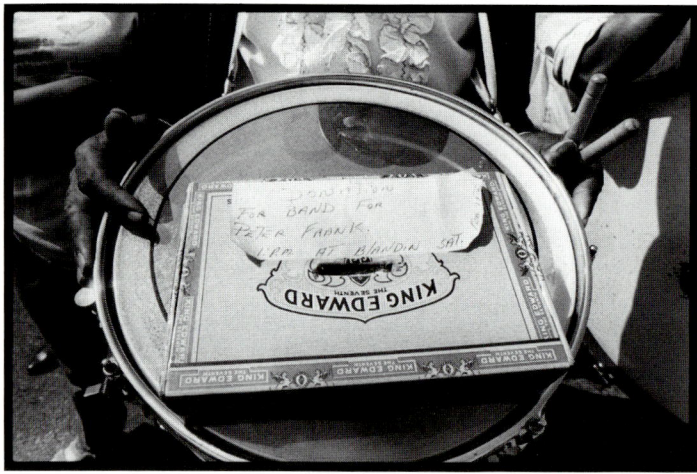

Donation for band, Peter Frank funeral   2184/12   1983

one white guy into it and he's a Rhodes scholar or something at the University of California. He's all right. I have no problem with that.

I'm Chief of the Golden Star Hunters. I worked my way up from Chief Scout to First Spy to Big Chief. The only one who has me beat in years on the street is Tootie Montana. If I make it this year, it will be my eighteenth straight year. A lot of people don't have that strength.

The purpose of the Council of Indians was to let people know that the black Mardi Gras Indians were organized, to help people get a better understanding. The Council consists of Uptown and Downtown Indians. And that is something you never used to see, an Uptown Indian associating with a Downtown Indian. The Council works to get more people in, get the children involved, which is kind of hard because of the expense. The Council is trying to write a book this year—a history of the Mardi Gras Indians. It's the first time that blacks ever put that information together. For a long time, everybody else was writing, but not the blacks.

A Celebration of New Orleans Music

Dave "Fat Man" Williams' funeral   2056/4   1982

Gate Johnson funeral with the Scene Boosters Social & Pleasure Club and the Dirty Dozen Brass Band   2213/32   1983

A Celebration of New Orleans Music

Danny and Lu Barker   2172/9-10   1983

Pin Stripe Brass Band, Olympian Aide Club parade   2185/10   1983

A Celebration of New Orleans Music

Treme Sports Social and Pleasure Club annual parade   2127/34   1982

A Joyful Noise

Big Joe Turner at the New Orleans Jazz & Heritage Festival   2190/21   1983

Professor Gizmo (Rick Elmore) One-Man-Band
2192/31A   1983

A Celebration of New Orleans Music

Buddy Guy and Jr. Wells at the New Orleans Jazz & Heritage Festival   2194/31   1983

The Holy Family, the Holy Family Spiritual Church   1070/5   1974

Archbishop Lydia Gilford

(Infant Jesus of Prague Spiritual Church of Christ)

All I say is to each his own. Whatever you like, you like. Whatever I like, I like. I've got nothing to do with that. Watson likes some things that I don't. I like some things that he don't. One Lord, one faith, and one baptism.

If the Indians serve God, they're serving him in spirit. This is a spirit God. See what I mean? While we are human, then we are serving him in Spirit, because the Bible says you can't see God and live.

The Lord spoke to me one day and told me to get the small people together. He didn't tell me to get the big dignitaries. Get the small people and let the small people try to do what God wants them to do. I feel that if you have somebody that's trying to help you and bring your gift out, well, that's the one you want to be around. You don't have to be like that big dignitary who isn't going to give you a chance. He's going to get the recognition. You see, we want the small people to get recognized, too. As an individual, you want to get recognized, you understand? But if you don't ever get recognized, you become somebody thrown over there in that corner. So, that's what I've been doing: trying to

A JOYFUL NOISE

"Spirit Dance" Infant Jesus of Prague Spiritual Church   1472/21A   1977

"In the Spirit" Infant Jesus of Prague Spiritual Church
1478/12A   1977

help the small individual, doing what God is telling me to do, and giving the individuals belief in themselves.

There's no secret about what God can do. What He has done for another, He can do for you. You've got to get that hope and desire, the will power, and the mind to do these things. Then God will bring you out. That's what I found down through the years. Now He says, "Where you find two or three assembled, there will be God in the midst." That means you don't have to have a big crowd to serve God. You've got three: God, you and me in every church. You see, we feel the presence. That's what I like about it, you see. But some people go for a crowd. There's danger in a crowd. That's why the small edifice gives more charisma than the large crowd which can be so cold. That's what I get out of it.

I know others don't run their churches like I run mine. I came out of the Catholic faith and mine is a mixture of Catholic and Baptist. I've been doing this for twenty-four years, so I ain't going to change. I'm fifty-nine now and if my folks try to change, I tell them, "Uh-uh, we don't do it like that." That's the size of that.

In Houston we have prayer rooms. We have prayer. They don't want congregations. They'd rather just have prayer and visit. You see, everybody is not called a pastor. You have to be called to pastor. Then you can weather the storm because you've got to go through some changes when you pastor. That's right. You've got to know if the people are light or heavy because you can get some spirits in here and they are mean, and boy, I tell you, you catch it if you don't know what to do for them.

I started in my front room where I had to knock the wall down and push it back. Finally, I had the whole five-room house the congregation built up. I did what God told me to do. That's how I started. I've been with God ever since. I don't know any other way.

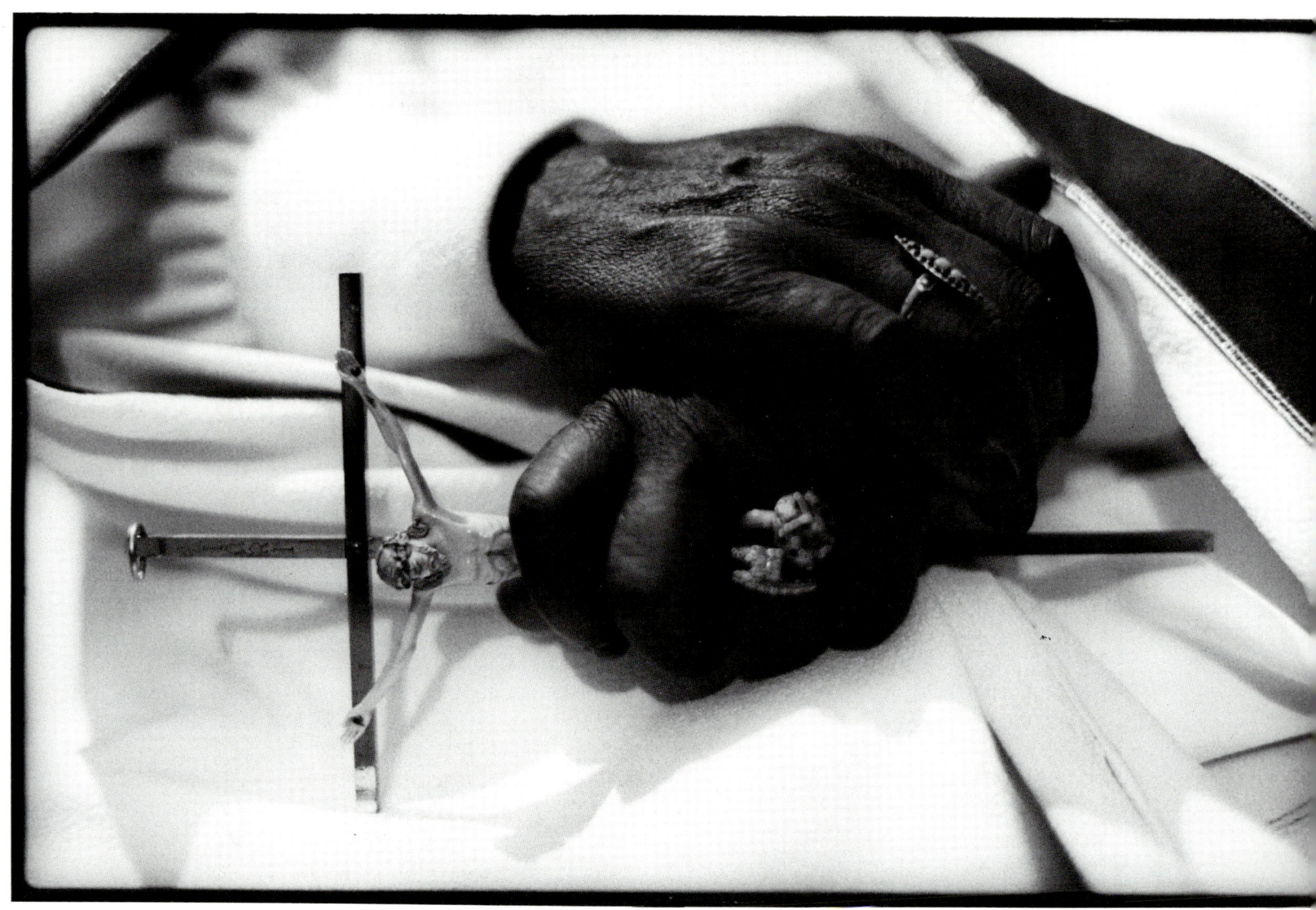

"Healing Hands": Bishop H. Brooks visiting Infant Jesus of Prague Spiritual Church   1263/9   1975

A Celebration of New Orleans Music

Reverend Mother Lydia Gilford   224/11   1973

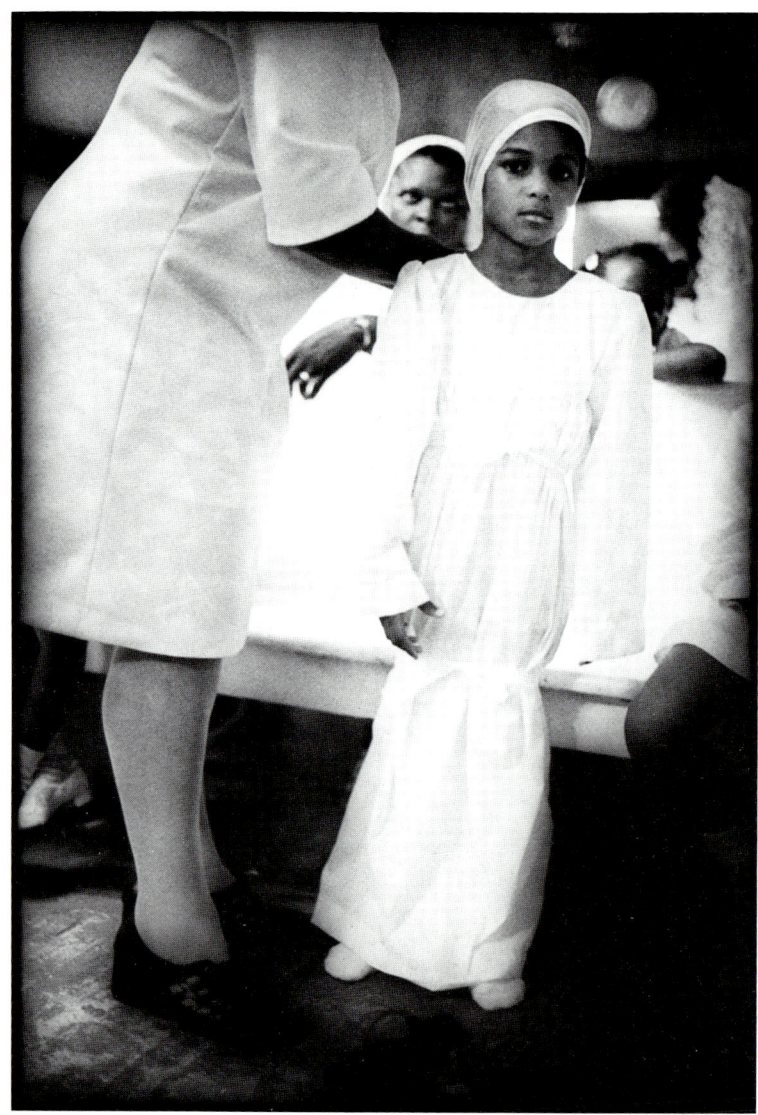

Binding for baptism, Holy Family Spiritual Church   937/30   1973

A Celebration of New Orleans Music

Baptism in Mirror, Reverend Mother Gilford presiding, Israelite Universal Divine Spiritual Church   975/23A   1973

Deacon Frank Lastie on drums at the Guiding Star Spiritual Church   1001/20   1973

A Celebration of New Orleans Music

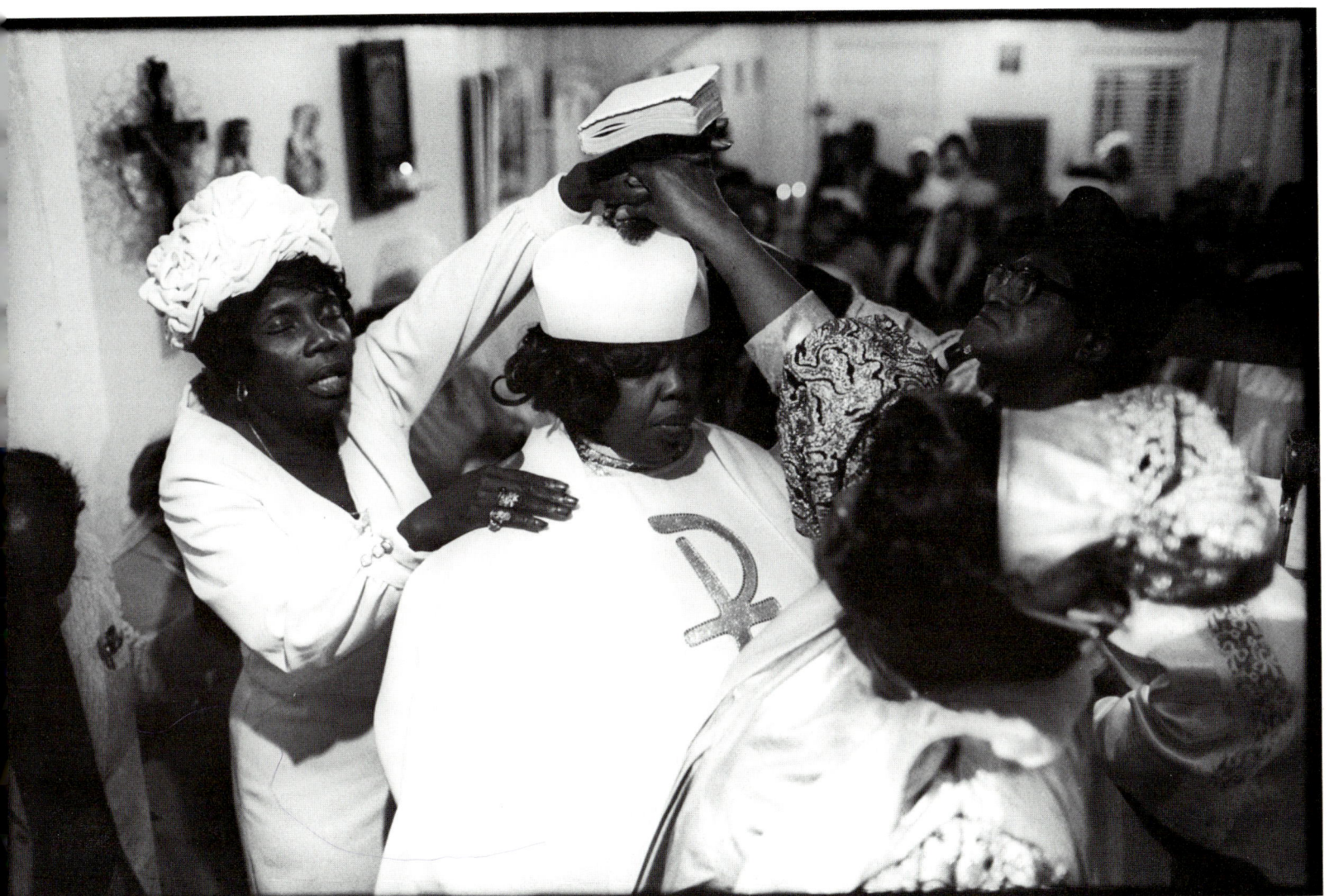

Ordination of Bishop Lydia Gilford   1036/9   1974

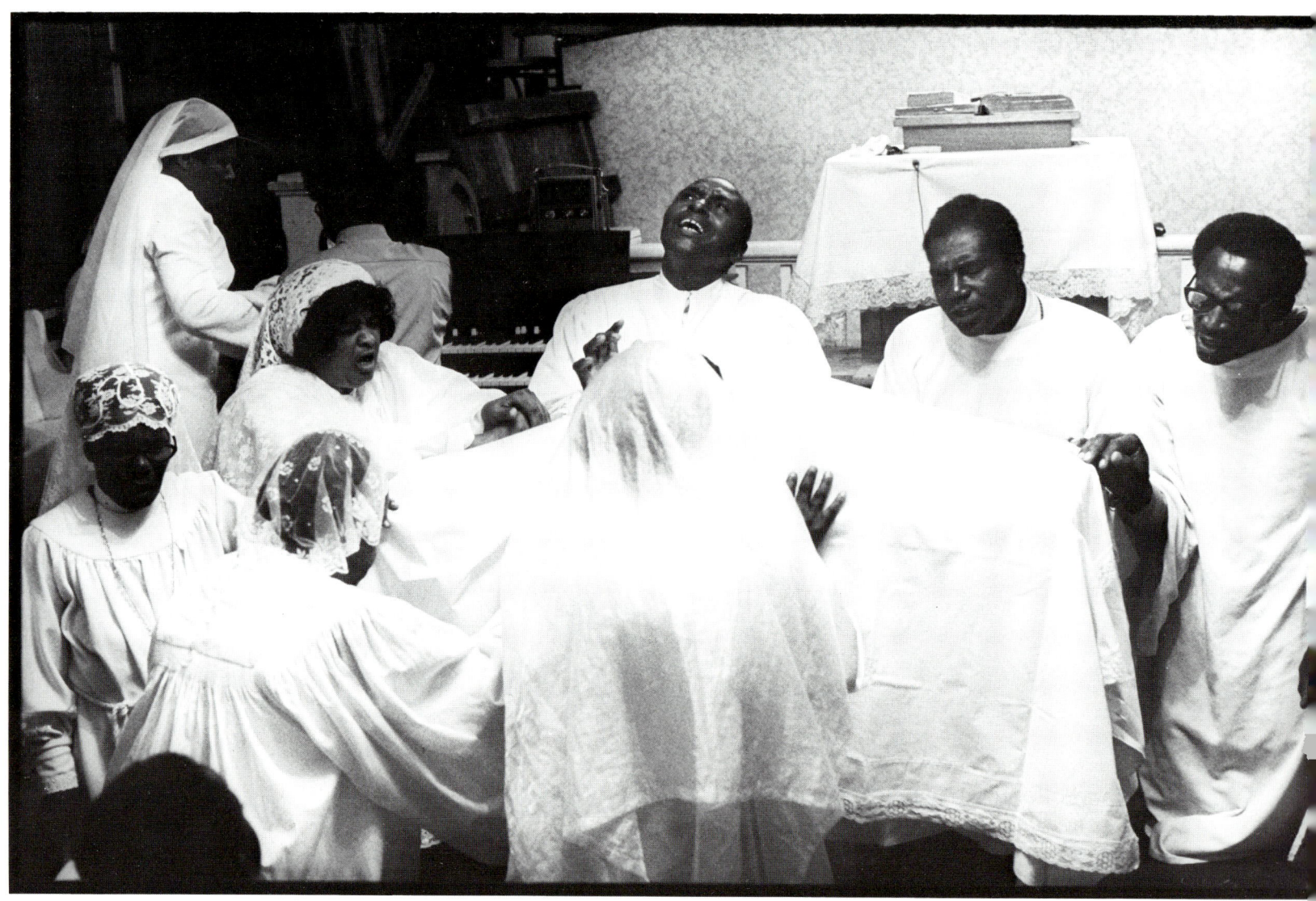

Praying over "the body of Christ," the Holy Spiritual Church   935/22   1973

Archbishop E.J. Johnson

(Israel Universal Divine Spiritual Churches of Christ)

As far as I know, our church is like any other so far as services are concerned. We believe in the Baptism, and the Communion, which is essential to the church. A lot of people have different theories of worship. We're criticized a lot of times. They say we worship idols. Of course, we honor certain saints, but we are not worshipping idols. According to the Scripture, the saints are going to judge the world. The Scripture says, "So a man lives. So he dies." And these saints that we honor, they are a help. One thing some people don't understand is that the body dies and the spirit doesn't. What a person carries on in life he also carries it on in the spirit after he is dismissed from the body.

    We believe in altars and we believe in honoring the saints. We believe that the Holy Spirit can help you if you pray and ask for help. We make sacrifices and offer them lights and offer them whatever we feel is necessary. We have feasts honoring saints, such as St. Anthony and St. Joseph. This is part of our ritual.

    We honor Blackhawk, who was the Indian warrior. The folks who honor him believe that he is a help to them if they ask him for help. They honor Blackhawk and Whitehawk and Sitting Bull, major spirits in their lives who are known to grant

Ordination service at the Israelite Universal Divine Spiritual Church, the hour of midnight   2117/37   1982

your petition for things. That's what it's all about. All of this is done through faith. So a man believes, so it is.

I've been in the Spiritual Church for about sixty years. I was nineteen or twenty years old at that time. When I came into this church, I was christened Catholic. My family? Part were Catholic, part were Protestant. After I grew up I didn't attend the Catholic church. I attended the Protestant church, but I didn't really connect until I connected with the Spiritual Church.

When I visited the Spiritual Church for the first time, I had an afflicted arm. My arm was swollen. For two weeks I had been unable to use it. The first time I went they prayed for me and laid a hand on my arm, and the next day my arm was normal as it's supposed to be. From there, I picked up faith and began following until I was converted to that because that's the way I wanted to be. That's how I got into it. That's where I've been ever since.

I started with Mamie Reison. From there I went to Reverend J.J. Johnson. I took my schooling under him and I was ordained under him in 1927 as a pastor. During that time I began running the service, but we were in rented halls and things like that. I did that for three years and then in 1930 I bought a church called Israelite Spiritual Church at 631 South Roman Street. We stayed there thirty-five, maybe forty years, until the highway came and took that. We got this church in May of 1970.

Some of the Spiritualist churches have different methods of worshipping. It's a little hard to explain because I don't go around to too many. At most of the churches I am affiliated with, we are all on the same wavelength. We worship almost the same. Some folks claim they have different ideas about worshipping, but I can't think too much about that.

In my organization we've got about thirty-five different churches in New Orleans, but there are others in Illinois, Ohio, Michigan, Texas. They are scattered around and they are grouped under the Israel Universal Divine Spiritual Churches of Christ.

The way some other churches go about it, a lot of people say they're talking to the dead. But when you're prophesying or healing, you go through the spirit of God. The dead can't do a thing for you.

A Joyful Noise

Jimmy the Hawk funeral   2253/27   1983

Ordination of Bishops at the Israelite Universal Divine Spiritual Church   2223/5   1983

A Celebration of New Orleans Music

Sister Catherine   225/12   1974

One of the big problems we have had with the Spiritual Church is that there is another group that says it's Spiritualist. Some claim that when you're Spiritualist you are without the spirit. But we are not without the spirit. We call ourselves Spiritual as a denomination. But all churches are in a sense spiritual churches because that is the only way you can worship God—in spirit and in truth. There is no other way.

Every year the Social and Pleasure clubs have a religious service and then they go about their parade and have their dance or whatever they are going to have. They always pick a church to go to. They don't go to the same church all the time. A couple of my members belong to the Social and Pleasure clubs.

What is done in the clubs depends on the individual and is judged by the church and community on an individual basis. It's what the individual does with the club that matters.

At one time there was a great division among the churches but that division has closed up quite a bit. It used to be that Protestants did not go to the Catholic Church, and the Catholic people weren't supposed to go to Protestant churches. It was considered a sin. But now Protestants and Catholics mix with Baptists and those who go to the Spiritual Church. That's begun to change over the last nine years. The Catholic church changed itself a lot. Now they have spiritual choirs that sing the same songs that we sing, but before they didn't do that.

Most of the Protestants didn't believe in healing or prophesying or tarrying for the Holy Ghost. They're stressing healing. So when we came along we'd have drums and tambourines and things like that in the church and we were severely criticized for it. But now most of the churches have drums and tambourines and the other things we were criticized for. Some churches have whole bands.

Frank Lastie was a member of this church and his whole family were musicians—piano, cornet, saxophone, right here. He'd gather the best musicians he could to play in the church. It was accepted here, but it wasn't elsewhere.

So we were not that far out after all because these things are supposed to be. This helps the community become tighter. The affiliations are better.

In St. Louis we had problems with the police arresting the Spiritual people as fortune-tellers. What would happen is that a couple of policewomen would go

A Celebration of New Orleans Music

The Avenue Steppers annual banner blessing parade   2392/19   1985

around to the different services and next thing you know the police would come and arrest the ministers. This happened to one of our churches. I was with Metropolitan and, at the time the lady got arrested, she had a church in the house. It was a two-room concern. What they'd do, they'd arrest these church people and the people would have to pay a hundred dollars and they would let them out. Then they'd go get somebody else. So when this lady got arrested, we asked for a trial. Then we came from the South, North, and everywhere so that we crowded the courthouse. And when the judge came out he wanted to know who all of these people were. That's why togetherness means something. Well, the lawyer said these are the bishops, ministers, and congregations from various places. So he dismissed the jury. And these policewomen who had accused this lady of being a fortune-teller, the judge called them up and asked them if they had visited Minister Davis' church. Asked them, "Was there a rostrum, like a pulpit?" And they said, "Yes."

Then the judge asked, "Did they get a prophecy? Did she charge anything?"

"No, she just asked for a donation."

And the judge dismissed that trial and that hasn't happened there since.

I'm eighty-one. I'll be eighty-two on December 26, the day after Christmas. My congregation has about a hundred and fifty members. Membership has dropped off. This is part of the Scripture, too. It says, "In the latter day there will be a falling away from the church," and nobody has services like they used to have. We used to have services three and four times a week. Now we are doing good if we have two services. People just don't come. Their excuse is that they're afraid to travel. We don't have services anymore at night. We used to have a service from seven o'clock to one or two in the morning, but now we're lucky if we can get service to last to ten. The economy has something to do with it and people are afraid to walk the streets. People used to walk the streets at night, but folks won't do that anymore. There have to be three or four or five of them together to go out there and catch a bus or streetcar to go home at nine or ten o'clock at night.

We've been called "voodoos" and "hoodoos," but that's not from what people knew, but from what they heard somebody say, but we pay that no mind.

They don't understand. We pray for people. We set lights for people and things like that and they brand us as hoodoo.

There are other churches affiliated with this church. We have tried to unify our forces as much as we possibly can with the same doctrine and services. We wanted to conduct services in the same manner. The congregations still visit each other, but not in bulk like we used to. Now when we go, we may have ten or twelve people, or maybe five or six. At one time we'd have a whole choir and the ushers. It's not like that now because if you do get a good group to go, you've got to provide transportation. Years ago, we could walk from one church to another, but you can't get people to do that anymore. If you get them there and take them back, they'll go, but if they have to provide their own transportation, then they can't. A lot of them don't have their own cars. We are still affiliated, it's just on a smaller scale.

We have quite a few young people. Most of the people who belong to the church have kids. So kids go most times with their parents. We have quite a few kids who have grown up to be adults in the church. When one group grows up, another comes along.

What I'm trying to do is to unify the churches more than they really are. They're like many denominations, where you have a lot of little organizations that are scattered about. We want to bring them together into a major organization.

They were taught to keep politics out of the church but they're learning differently now because politics affects how the people live. Most times now the candidates go and make speeches in the different churches. The church doesn't endorse candidates, but it does make a difference. The church is more involved in politics now than it ever was.

Religion is togetherness. A lot of organizations, a lot of ministers, instead of preaching togetherness, they have preached separation. They try to put one group against the other group, and it shouldn't be that way. We don't all worship in the same way, but I still shouldn't condemn you because you've got your way and I've got mine.

The New Orleans "Backbeat," Mt. Moriah Missionary Baptist Church annual parade   1754/18   1979

A Celebration of New Orleans Music

"Ironing Board Same" in Jackson Square   1583/7   1978

Bongo Joe, New Orleans Jazz & Heritage Festival
1609/22   1978

Mac Rebennack at Tipitina's   2195/10A   1983

A Celebration of New Orleans Music

Ernie K-Doe at the New Orleans Jazz & Heritage Festival   2192/25A   1983

Bobby Bland at the
New Orleans Jazz &
Heritage Festival
2306/8A   1984

A Celebration of New Orleans Music

Chester Jones funeral   2340/19   1984

The Dixie Cups with Aaron Neville at the New Orleans Jazz & Heritage Festival   2373/29A   1984

A Celebration of New Orleans Music

Katie Webster at the
New Orleans Jazz &
Heritage Festival
2299/13   1984

The Pin Stripe Brass Band at the Jolly Bunch Social & Pleasure Club annual parade   2342/27   1984

A Celebration of New Orleans Music

Avenue Steppers Marching Club annual banner blessing parade   2101/4   1982

A JOYFUL NOISE

Stevie Ray Vaughan at the New Orleans Jazz & Heritage Festival   2460/25A   1986

Willie Dixon at the New Orleans Jazz & Heritage Festival
2375/13   1984

182

A Celebration of New Orleans Music

Sippie Wallace at the New Orleans Jazz & Heritage Festival   2375/20   1984

The All Stars Jazz Band in Jackson Square, New Orleans   2382/12   1985

A Celebration of New Orleans Music

Avenue Steppers' annual parade   2205/19   1983

A JOYFUL NOISE

Dancing in the rain, Young Men's Olympian annual parade, 5th Division   2413/26   1985

A Celebration of New Orleans Music

Spencer Coudray's funeral, member of Young Men Olympian Jr. Benevolent Association   2265/16A   1983

Al Green at the New Orleans Jazz & Heritage Festival   2200/21   1983

A Celebration of New Orleans Music

Earl King with Stevie Ray Vaughan at the New Orleans Jazz & Heritage Festival   2464/18   1986

Chief Walter Cook (Creole Wild West Mardi Gras Indian tribe) and family, Mardi Gras Day   2446/6   1986

A Celebration of New Orleans Music

Spencer Coudray's funeral, Young Men Olympian Benevolent Association   2270/14   1983

Spencer Coudray's funeral, Young Men Olympian Benevolent Association   2268/30   1983

A Celebration of New Orleans Music

The Olympia Jr. Brass Band at Pork Chop's funeral   2477/5   1986

Lady B.J., Wanda Rouzan, and Monis Jeff at Ellyna Tatum's funeral   2515/30   1986

A Celebration of New Orleans Music

Rebirth Jazz Band at the Sudan Club annual parade   2530/2   1986

A Joyful Noise

At the Sudan Club annual parade   2777/29   1988

Oliver "Pork Chop" Anderson at Harold Dudley funeral   2400/19   1985

A Celebration of New Orleans Music

Mardi Gras Indian on N. Clairborne   2187/7   1983

Wynton Marsalis and friend at the New Orleans Jazz & Heritage Festival   2839/31   1989

A Celebration of New Orleans Music

Miles Davis at the New Orleans Jazz & Heritage Festival   2852/15   1989

A Joyful Noise

Professor Longhair at the New Orleans Jazz & Heritage Festival 2567/36 1987

Charmaign Neville and friends—Rita Coolidge and sister at the New Orleans Jazz & Heritage Festival 2842/21 1989

200

A Celebration of New Orleans Music

The Buckjumpers parade   2866/16   1989

A Personal Statement from the Photographer

"A culturally diverse society based upon the principle of individual rights must be a society dedicated to the conservation of cultures—for culture at every level is the imaginative medium, the body of codes and conventions, of signs and signals, dreams and fancies, in which we have our individuality. We have seen what happens to a people when they are robbed of their way of life, and how utterly nugatory is the idea of individual rights when there is no culture in and through which to exercise them."

Robert Cantwell, The Midway on the Mall:
Twenty Years of the Festival of American Folklife

The traditional culture presented in A Joyful Noise is a vast, organic, cultural system not recognized or protected for its intrinsic spiritual and social merit, or as a potential economic resource. Municipal authorities are largely ignorant of the historic values and creativity it represents and don't understand how the city inadvertently contributes to its oppression and decline.

Today, because this culture is so obscure, and so deeply submerged in the inner city, it is not properly understood by outsiders for its function in the community as an essential spiritual fountainhead which continually revitalizes authentic African-American expressive arts, and which makes seminal contributions to the unique quality and authenticity of New Orleans' world-renowned music.

Historically, the second-line parades and street culture of New Orleans were an expression of independence. Brass band parades developed early in the black community and were always associated with the cause of black freedom

and political advancement. P.B.S. Pinchback, acting black governor of Louisiana during Reconstruction (1872/73), reflecting on the social situation of the time and its relation to groups that formed and sponsored early black bands, advised: "Form Societies of Benevolence... hold meetings at least once a week to debate the questions of the day, that relate directly to us thus keeping the masses posted on what is going on." (Schafer & Allen, *Brass Bands & New Orleans Jazz*: L.S.U. Press, 1977). Schafer & Allen continued, "...We do know that the excitement and social change accompanying Reconstruction nourished the black brass band tradition in New Orleans. The stimulus of emancipation, the prolonged presence of Federal troops and military bands in the city, the promise of social and political equality for black people contributed to the style and content of the music. Much like the spirituals and jubilees of slavery times, this band music was born of an intense, emotionally charged desire for freedom and recognition. Its militancy is not of the battlefield or of the church, but of the political arena; and it reflects the great expectations of black people in the years following their official release from bondage."

It is ironic that these traditional societies and sociopolitical clubs, now popularly known as the second-line marching clubs, are still struggling to realize the freedoms and recognition they should have gained as a result of the Civil War. It is a great loss to all of us that African-American culture was not allowed to develop naturally in ways which might contribute to improvement in the circumstances of their own community, as well as society at large.

African-Americans, for example, supported and nurtured jazz as an integral part of their traditional culture long before the city's leadership recognized its value as an important economic resource, and began to develop jazz in ways which would primarily benefit the city. Now municipal authorities forget the cultural ancestry of jazz. They herald jazz as a great, living New Orleans attraction, but fail to protect and nourish its traditional cultural roots. Furthermore, the city has not allowed the community which created jazz to develop and nurture it in their own way so it could maintain a natural vitality and continue its seminal contributions to the authentic music of the city.

Louis Armstrong remembered the parades from his earliest years, shortly

A Celebration of New Orleans Music

after the turn of the century: "To watch those clubs parade was an irresistible and absolutely unique experience... I had spent my life in New Orleans, but every time one of those clubs paraded I would second-line them all day long. By carrying the cornet for Joe Oliver or Bunk Johnson I would get enough to eat to hold me until the parade was over." Armstrong also commented about a later period in his development: "The fact that I belonged to the best brass band in town put me in touch with all the top musicians..." It is clear how and where Louis Armstrong learned his music.

Very few traditional jazz greats from New Orleans did not begin their careers in the streets playing for the second-line parades. Buddy Bolden, Sidney Bechet, Edward "Kid" Ory, Freddie Keppard, "Jelly Roll" Morton, Oscar "Papa" Celestin, "Big Eye Louis" Nelson, and others were all involved with and clearly influenced by the second-line parade tradition. The spectacular annual parades continuing today are an integral part of the distinctive history and roots of New Orleans jazz. These parades highlight the authentic context of our living jazz heritage.

The Mardi Gras Indian gangs and Spiritual churches of New Orleans presented in A *Joyful Noise* are additional cultural treasures deserving special recognition. They are classic examples of historic cultures quietly serving the spiritual needs and interests of a tightly knit traditional community, carrying on and preserving a complex music, art, and culture, under the most difficult circumstances.

I have commented extensively on the cultural contributions of the vernacular churches and black "Indian" gangs to New Orleans in my book *Spirit World*. The black "Indian" gangs are the oldest cultural organizations surviving from the original African tribes which were brought into New Orleans during the slavery days, and are now widely recognized for preserving African-American culture, dress art, and musical heritage in the New World. It was the African drumming traditions and music concepts preserved within these gangs which combined with the military brass marching band tradition in the streets of New Orleans during the latter half of the nineteenth century which led to the development of Jazz. Also, the sewing and beadwork in their costumes, which are dismantled and redesigned each year, are widely regarded to be one of the finest examples of traditional African-American folk art in North America.

A Joyful Noise

The beat and lyrics of the gangs, beyond their contribution to the development of jazz, have inspired the music of Jelly Roll Morton, Smiley Lewis, Sugarboy Crawford, Guitar Slim, Professor Longhair, James Booker, Mac Rebenack, Fats Domino, the Neville Brothers, and countless others. If you pick the memories of almost any musician raised in New Orleans—whether Jazz, Blues, Rhythm & Blues, Rock 'N' Roll, or Rap—you will inevitably end up talking about second-line parades, jazz funerals, neighborhood live-music clubs, vernacular churches, and the Mardi Gras Indian gangs (the five basic elements of New Orleans music).

Although New Orleans is now well-known for its music, the second-line celebrations and other traditional cultural activity in the community, taken as a whole, are an astonishing example of New Orleans' living cultural riches which are largely overlooked. But it is these traditional cultural elements which comprise the foundation of our city's unique character and music. Now, because of neglect and inadvertent municipal repression, we are in the process of losing this extraordinary heritage... and the historic quality of our music as well.

Despite chilling changes in the nature of our society, the past twenty years have brought hope to all of us who are working to bring recognition and protection to our cultural heritage. Louisiana's unique folk traditions are well on their way to becoming recognized as one of our state's great natural resources, and potentially a vast unexplored economic resource. Furthermore, the political process which leads to protection and encouragement of our diverse cultures is well under way.

In recent years folklorists and cultural activists have tried to do more than describe culture. They are now contributing to the empowerment of folk communities, and are offering their expertise in research, cooperative planning, and documentation as tools to be utilized by the community for self-determination and internal development. Today the foremost concern of academic professionals in this field is to insure that traditional, isolated, and/or oppressed folk communities are properly recognized for all their spiritual and material contributions to our society, that they are not traumatized by outside authorities and economic forces, that they be well documented and studied so as to preserve their unique storehouse of information, and that they receive their fair share of the economic benefits which might derive from their unique creations and productions.

If New Orleans could find ways to protect, encourage, and make visible the stylistic and cultural variety that makes life in New Orleans unique, the city could easily become the Mecca for cultural-heritage tourism in the United States, and the results of this could be of profit to everyone. The primary benefits from the presentation of this culture, though, should flow into the community preserving this heritage and presenting these spectacular celebrations. Properly done, this could bring about a great flowering period for cultural diversity in New Orleans which would greatly enrich all our lives.

What is shown in this work is only a small part of the cultural celebration to be enjoyed in The Creole City. Space limitation permits only a representative selection of images. My apologies to the many individual performers and important cultural organizations not mentioned or included.

My intent, in this selection of views from the inside, is to show our music and culture in its vital organic context, so that New Orleans can be seen, understood, and appreciated by all as one of North America's most vibrant and inspiring cultural wellsprings.

Michael P. Smith

Selected Bibliography

Armstrong, Louis. *Satchmo: My Life in New Orleans*. New York: Prentice-Hall, 1954.

Ashforth, Alden. Liner notes for *Doc Paulin's Marching Band*. Folkways FS 2856.

Bannock, Larry. Interviews with Alan Govenar. New Orleans, July 21 and September 14, 1988.

Berry, Jason; Foose, Jonathan; and Jones, Tad. *Up From the Cradle of Jazz: New Orleans Music Since World War II*. Athens, Georgia: University of Georgia Press, 1986.

Blassingame, John W. *Black New Orleans, 1860-1880*. Chicago: University of Chicago Press, 1973.

Brock, Jerry. Liner notes for *The Chosen Few*. Syla AL-349.

———. Liner notes for *Here To Stay*, The Rebirth Jazz Band. Arhoolie 1092.

Broven, John. *Rhythm and Blues in New Orleans*. Gretna, Louisiana: Pelican Publishing, 1978.

Buerkle, Jack V., and Barker, Danny. *Bourbon Street Black*. New York: Oxford University Press, 1973.

Charters, Samuel B. Liner notes for *The Music of the Eureka Brass Band*. Folkways FA 2462.

———. *Jazz New Orleans, 1885-1963*. New York: Oak Publications, 1963.

Dejan, Harold. Interview with Alan Govenar. New Orleans, December 11, 1988.

Dent, Tom. "A Memoir of Mardi Gras, 1968." *Black River Journal* (1980): 14-16.

Francis, Sylvester. Interview with Alan Govenar. New Orleans, July 22, 1988.

Hannusch, Jeff. *I Hear You Knockin': The Sound of New Orleans Rhythm and Blues*. Ville Platte, Louisiana: Swallow Publications, 1985.

Jacobs, Claude F. "Benevolent Societies of New Orleans During the Late Nineteenth and Early Twentieth Century." *Louisiana History* 29 (1988): 22.

———. "Spirit Guides and Possession in the New Orleans Black Spiritual Churches." *Journal of American Folklore* 102 (January-March 1989): 45-67.

Kaslow, Allison. "Mardi Gras Indians." *Louisiana Folklore Miscellany* 3 (1972): 48-49.

Kaslow, Andrew. *Oppression and Adaptation: The Social Organization and Expressive Culture in New Orleans*. New York: Columbia University Press, 1981.

———, and Jacobs, Claude. "Prophecy, Healing and Power: The Afro-American Spiritual Churches in New Orleans." *Report for the Jean Lafitte National Historical Park* (1981).

Marquis, Don. *In Search of Buddy Bolden*. Baton Rouge: Louisiana State University Press, 1978.

Martinez, E., and Lecorgne, M. *Uptown/Downtown*. New Orleans: Center for Louisiana Studies, 1986.

McDonald, Robert R.; Kemp, John R.; and Haas, Edward F., eds. *Louisiana's Black Heritage*. New Orleans: Louisiana State Museum, 1979.

Montana, Allison. Interview with Alan Govenar. New Orleans, December 11, 1988.

Salaam, Kalamu Ya. Interview with Alan Govenar. New Orleans, September 15, 1988.

———. Liner notes for *Mardi Gras in Montreux*, The Dirty Dozen Brass Band. Rounder 2052.

———. "Musical Travelogues." *Wavelength* (September 1982): 39-41.

———. *Our Music Is No Accident*. New Orleans: New Orleans Cultural Foundation, 1988.

Schafer, William J. and Allen, Richard B. *Brass Bands and New Orleans Jazz*. Baton Rouge: Louisiana State University Press, 1977.

Smith, Michael P. *Spirit World*. New Orleans: Louisiana Committee for the Humanities, 1983.

Spitzer, Nicolas R., ed. *Louisiana Folklife*. Baton Rouge: Louisiana Folklife Program, Office of Cultural Development, Department of Culture, Recreation, and Tourism, 1985.

Stephenson, Johnny. Interview with Alan Govenar. New Orleans, September 14, 1988.